Sylvanus Cobb

The Storm Children

Or, The Light-Keeper of the Channel

Sylvanus Cobb

The Storm Children
Or, The Light-Keeper of the Channel

ISBN/EAN: 9783337180119

Printed in Europe, USA, Canada, Australia, Japan

Cover: Foto ©ninafisch / pixelio.de

More available books at **www.hansebooks.com**

THE STORM CHILDREN;

OR,

THE LIGHT-KEEPER OF THE CHANNEL.

A Story of Sea and Land Adventure.

BY SYLVANUS COBB, JR.

THE STORM CHILDREN IN DANGER.

BOSTON:
OFFICE BALLOU'S MONTHLY MAGAZINE.
G. W. STUDLEY, PUBLISHER, 23 HAWLEY ST.

THE NOVELETTE.

ENTERTAINING STORIES BY STANDARD AMERICAN AUTHORS,

ILLUSTRATED.

No. 1.—The Arkansas Ranger, or Dingle the Backwoodsman. A Story of East and West. By Lieut. Murray. A vivid story, unrivaled in plot and character; thrilling in marvelous adventures.

No. 2.—The Sea Lion, or The Privateer of the Penobscot. A Story of Ocean Life. By Sylvanus Cobb, Jr. One of Cobb's best; occurring during that fertile period of adventure, our second war with England.

No. 3.—Marion's Brigade, or The Light Dragoons. A Tale of the Revolution. By Dr. J. H. Robinson. Among the many tales which our Revolutionary struggles have drawn from the pens of noted historians and story-tellers, perhaps none excel this one from the pen of Dr. Robinson.

No. 4.—Bessie Baine, or the Mormon's Victim. A Tale of Utah. By M. Quad, of the Detroit Free Press. In this great original story, written expressly for our establishment, Mr. Lewis has shown up the whole system of Mormonism, and all its terrible aims and results.

No. 5.—The Red Revenger, or the Pirate King of the Floridas. A Tale of the Gulf and its Islands. By Ned Buntline. This thrilling tale is one that portrays many tragic and romantic phases of life at a period when deadly conflict was maintained between the Spaniards of Cuba and the desperate pirates who infested the seas in its vicinity some three centuries ago.

No. 6.—Orlando Chester, or The Young Hunter of Virginia. A Story of Colonial Times. By Sylvanus Cobb, Jr. This story is one of the happiest efforts of the author, who has wrought out a series of domestic scenes in private life of much interest.

No. 7.—The Secret-Service Ship, or the Fall of San Juan d'Ulloa. A Romance of the Mexican War. By Capt. Charles E. Averill. The author enjoyed extraordinary facilities for gaining the actual knowledge necessary to the production of this captivating story; and hence its truthfulness and excellence.

No. 8.—Adventures in the Pacific, or In Chase of a Wife. By Col. Isaac H. Folger. This sea story will attract much attention from residents of the Cape, and many old whaling captains and crews will recall its characters and incidents with lively interest, and all fond of adventure will read it with relish.

No. 9.—Ivan the Serf, or the Russian and Circassian. A Tale of Russia, Turkey, and Circassia. By Austin C. Burdick. This is a well-told and highly graphic tale of life, domestic and military, in Russia, Turkey, and Circassia.

No. 10.—The Scout, or the Sharpshooters of the Revolution. A Story of our Revolutionary Struggle. By Major Ben. Perley Poore. This story of our Revolutionary struggle is one of much interest, and narrates, with vivid, lifelike effect, some of the scenes of that eventful period.

No. 11.—Daniel Boone, or The Pioneers of Kentucky. A Tale of Early Western Life. By Dr. J. H. Robinson. The terrible experiences of the early Western settlers, with their perils and privations, their struggles, and their triumphs, afford a vivid field for the writer, who has lent himself to the task with a rich result.

No. 12.—The King of the Sea. A Tale of the Fearless and Free. By Ned Buntline. This is one of the most popular romances of the sea written by this well-known author, and the characters which appear are replete with interest and individuality.

No. 13.—The Queen of the Sea, or Our Lady of the Ocean. A Tale of Love and Chivalry. By Ned Buntline. This is a story of the buccaneers of the seventeenth century, and is fraught with the sanguinary incidents of those times.

No. 14.—The Heart's Secret, or The Fortunes of a Soldier. A Tale of Love and the Low Latitudes. By Lieutenant Murray. This is a very interesting story of life among the noble in the island of Cuba. Its plot is well conceived and happily carried out, and furnishes a skillful series of events of intense interest.

No. 15.—The Storm Children, or The Light-Keeper of the Channel. A Story of Land and Sea Adventure. By Sylvanus Cobb, Jr. This story is one of great interest. The principal incidents are located on the coast of England, although the developments carry the reader into the Eastern world. It is a fine portraiture of human character.

ANNOUNCEMENT.

Novelette Number Sixteen will be ready for publication about October 16th, containing the following story:

ONE-EYED JAKE;

OR, THE YOUNG DRAGOON.

A Story of the Revolutionary Struggle.   BY EDWARDS KEELER OLMSTEAD.

All persons well read in the literature of our country are familiar with Cooper's novel, "The Spy." This novel, though less in extent, is based upon scenes like those employed by Cooper. The author has portrayed them in a masterly manner, fully equalling in intensity the work of the great novelist.

A New Book is Issued Each Month.

☞ For sale at all periodical depots throughout the country, or sent by mail, post-paid by the publisher, on receipt of 15 cents per copy; or will send Four Books for 50 cents; Eight Books, $1.00, all post-paid.

G. W. STUDLEY, 23 HAWLEY STREET, BOSTON, MASS.

THE STORM CHILDREN;

— OR, —

THE LIGHT-KEEPER OF THE CHANNEL.

A Story of Sea and Land Adventure.

BY SYLVANUS COBB, JR.

THE STORM CHILDREN IN DANGER.

CHAPTER I.

THE LIGHT-KEEPER AND HIS PROTEGE.

UPON the nothern coast of Devonshire, some seven miles to the west of the confines of Somerset, there makes out into the British Channel an abrupt promontory, known sometimes among seamen as Little Devon Head. From its north-eastern point around to the eastern main, the shore is a smooth beach, while the nothern and western bounds are of ragged rocks. To the northeast, and shielding the little beach from the gales that come up from the Atlantic, a huge rock reaches out into the water, forming a small, snug cove, which lies unusually quiet with its still water, while the huge waves are lashing the rocks upon the opposite side of the promontory. From this cove a narrow path leads up on to the grass-grown summit of the headland, and there stands a small, one-story house, and near it is a beacon. The house and the beacon, at the time of which we write, were the only buildings upon the promontory. Back of the house, to the south, the view was cut off by a sturdy growth of oak, but to the north the scene was grand. Almost the whole surface of the British Channel could be swept with the naked eye, and the Welsh coast of Glamorgon was dimly visible in the distance.

It was about the middle of the afternoon of a day in early spring. In the little cove just alluded to, lay a large, sloop-built boat, with high, strong bulwarks, and short, stout spars. Near her bows stood a man who seemed, from his manner, to be the monarch of all about him. He was about forty years of age; he might have been older, and perhaps younger—but a shrewd calculator would have set him at forty, and the variation could not have been of much consequence. He was a strong-built man—his limbs all rightly shaped and proportioned, and set with an easy firmness. He wore a rough drab pea jacket, a coarse blue vest, and trowsers of heavy duck, while his head was covered with a wide-rimmed, low, bowl-crowned, painted hat. His brow was broad and heavy, his eyes black and large, his nose slightly Roman and prominent, and his mouth of a medium size. The lips were peculiar—being thinner than seemed to correspond with the other features, and seemed to be constantly quivering—a quivering, however, almost imperceptible, unless he was regarded somewhat particularly. His hair was short, leaving his broad brow and temples entirely bare, and its color was of a jetty black. His beard was of the same color, and it grew just where nature had provided, but it was neatly trimmed at the ends, nevertheless. The moustache swept off in a graceful curve on either side, leaving the marked lip in sight; and the whole beard was what would have been thought a "celestial possession" by a Persian monarch.

Such was Luke Garron, the light-keeper of the Devon Head. He stood now with one hand resting on the rail of the boat, and the other folded against his hip. The hand that rested on the hip drew back the front of the long jacket, and revealed a large pistol that reposed within the belt that supported the trowsers. By the light-keeper's side stood a stout, steeled-fluked grappling-hook and a heavy axe, implements which had on more than one occasion helped him in rendering assistance to those who needed it.

Luke Garron seemed fitted by nature to some higher sphere than that in which we now find him, but he was, nevertheless, just the man for the place he filled. Fearless and undaunted, strong, and persevering, generous and kind-hearted, he had saved many a life from the grave of the channel.

While standing as we have described him, he seemed lost in reflective thought, but ere long he was aroused by the appearance of a boy who came running down the path from the house. The boy made his way to the boat and approached the light-keeper. He was a lovely child, with bright, sunny curls, large blue eyes, and a smiling, happy cast of countenance. Not over eight years could have rolled over his head.

"Ah! what now, Alfred?" asked the man, as he stretched forth his hands to greet the new-comer.

"Oh, I've come to find you. Old Nepsey wont talk with me, and I feel lonesome."

Luke Garron stooped and kissed the boy's white brow.

"Nepsey is a good woman, but she doesn't like to talk," he said.

"Oh yes she's good," the boy uttered.

"Yes; and she loves you, too. I have just been thinking about you, Alfred."

"Ah! and what did you think, father? It was something good, I hope."

"I was thinking that you would always stay with me, and be my child."

"How can I help it? You are my father," the boy returned, as Luke took him up in his stout arms. "You saved my life from the ugly sea when I was almost drowned. You've always been good to me —very good—a great deal better than the old father I had."

"I guess you don't remember much about your other father."

"Oh yes I do," Alfred said, with considerable animation. "I remember how he used to strike me, and you are always so good. Oh, I love you!"

As the boy ceased speaking, he placed his finger upon Luke's cheek and wiped off a large tear that stood there. For some moments the man was silent. He kissed Alfred again, and said:—

"You must study, Alfred. I left you in the house with your book. You should have got your lesson before you came out."

"Oh! I've got it all perfect—every word of it."

Luke looked incredulous.

"I have, certainly," the boy continued, seeming to comprehend the meaning of his protector's look.

"Well, well, I'll hear you recite it when I go in."

Luke placed the boy upon his feet, and then turned to haul in a rope that was hanging overboard.

"Father, just see those great big black clouds that are rising over the rock. I saw them before I came down here. Suppose we should have one of those dreadful storms?"

Luke Garron looked up over his head, and he saw that the boy had spoken the truth. Heavy clouds were rolling up into the heavens, and the waters of the channel were changed to a sable hue. Little spits of wind were flying in from the Atlantic, and the waves were gathering tiny crests of white foam. Luke took the boy by the hand, and left the boat. When he reached the summit of the bluff he saw that a real storm was brewing in the west.

"I trust all ships may be well clear of the lee shore," murmured the light-keeper.

Alfred looked up into his face, and he knew, from the shades he saw there, that danger might be expected. Ere long big raindrops began to fall, and the light-keeper and his protege started towards the house.

"Ah!" uttered Luke, "who is that going off through the woods?"

"Oh! I forgot," returned Alfred, as he gazed in the direction pointed out by Luke's finger. "It's a man that stopped to get a drink of water; but I didn't think he would stop all this time. Nepsey was getting the water for him when I came out."

"Why does he go away just as it begins to rain?"

"Perhaps he's in a hurry."

"Maybe," fell from Garron's lips, and he spoke not again until he reached the house.

Nepsey was just beginning to prepare for cooking the supper. She was a woman somewhere about fifty years old, with a look of shrewdness about her face; and though her features were far from comely, yet they were by no means repulsive. She had been a sort of a fixture to the house for over twenty years, having lived there with her husband, who had been a former keeper of the place, but whose death had given the berth to the present incumbent.

"Who was that man, Nepsey, that called here just now?" asked Luke.

"I don't know, sir," returned Nepsey.

"He remained some time."

"Yes sir."

"To rest, I suppose?"

"Y—e—es, sir," hesitatingly answered the old woman, as she arose from the fire she had just been kindling upon the hearth. "He said he would rest."

Nepsey glanced mysteriously at Alfred as she spoke, and then her gaze was fixed earnestly upon her master. Luke noticed her manner, and a dark shade passed over his face.

"What did he say, Nepsey?" he asked.

"He asked me about Alfred."

"Well, and what did you tell him?"

The woman was uneasy, and the evident perturbation of her master increased the difficulty. She hesitated for a moment, and then said:—

"I told him more than I ought; but he commenced by asking his questions so carelessly, and so common-place like, that I did not mistrust that he had any interest in the matter."

"And how do you know that he did have any interest in the matter?" quickly asked Luke, gazing earnestly into the woman's face.

"By the way he looked and acted after he

found out that Alfred was not your child, but that you took him from the water in a great storm four years ago."

"Did you tell him all this?"

"Yes."

"You ought not to have done it."

"I know it."

Luke Garron was silent for some moments. Alfred crept to his side and asked him what was the matter; but Luke gave him no answer.

"What sort of a looking man was he?" he at length asked of Nepsey.

"Not at all pleasant or agreeable after he had been here a spell, though he looked well enough when he first called. He looked half wolf and half snake."

At any other time Garron would have smiled at Nepsey's answer, but he felt not like it now.

"Had he any feature by which you could mark him?" he asked.

"Yes; three great scars on his face—one across his nose, one on his cheek, and one across his chin."

"What does it all mean, father?" asked the boy, as he got up into Luke's lap and put his arms about the keeper's neck. "What does it all mean?"

"Nothing, nothing, my child," said Garron, who seemed nervous and unhappy.

"Ah! father, you remember what you heard me read in my Bible yesterday?"

Luke gazed into the face of the boy without speaking.

"You know," continued Alfred, "we must not deceive each other. I know you have something. Do tell me what it is. Come, I'll be good?"

"O Alfred, you must not ask me!" bitterly exclaimed Luke. "Nepsey, you should not have told him; you should not have said a word."

"But I couldn't—I didn't know. He did not seem to be anyways concerned about the matter at first, and I'm sure I didn't think of harm. Don't blame me!"

"I wont blame you, Nepsey," uttered Luke; "but I'm sorry—sorry!"

The light-keeper found the boy's gaze fixed earnestly upon him as he spoke. Those large, blue eyes were shining with an earnest, liquid light, and the lips were trembling with fear.

"Alfred," Luke said, "do not be alarmed; I will protect you."

"But what is the danger? Who is that man?"

Garron looked steadily into the boy's face some time without speaking. At length he said:—

"It must have been he who was wrecked with you."

"My father?" cried Alfred, with a look of alarm.

"Yes."

"Oh! you will not let me go away with him?" urged the boy, clinging more closely to his protector. "You will keep me with you?"

"Yes, yes," returned Luke, folding the boy to his bosom. "Fear not. I know Marrok Pettrell, and he shall not have"——

The light-keeper hesitated, his face grew darker, and he was more agitated.

"Come, Alfred, get your book, and I will hear your lesson. Let this fear pass from your mind."

The boy thought his protector had banished all his own fear. He was not old enough to read those quivering signs that dwelt still upon Luke's face, and with a look of assured safety he ran for his book. His lesson had indeed been most faithfully committed, and while he was answering his kind teacher's questions, his young face was lighted up by the glow of youthful ardor. He was proud to learn.

Luke Garron heard the lesson through, but his task was a hard one. He saw that the boy's fears were in a measure quieted, and he strove hard to prevent any look or word of his own from renewing them.

"That's a noble boy!" he said, as he returned the book. "Keep on so, and you will be a happy man."

Luke Garron may have meant what he said; but it is certain that he shuddered when he thought of the boy's future.

CHAPTER II.

THE TEMPEST.—THE SIGNAL GUN.

IT had grown dark, and Garron had gone to light up the beacon. The rain came down in sweeping torrents, and the wind howled like a mad lion. The sea roared with terror in its deep-toned voice, and the great waves crashed like tumbling mountains as they broke in fury over the rocks of the promontory.

"This is a fearful night," uttered the light-keeper, as he entered the house and shook the rain from his long jacket. "God forbid that there be a vessel on our coast!"

"How the wind howls," said Nepsey, who was crouched away in the chimney corner. "It's never blown harder than this but once for twenty years; and that was when the sea rolled up over our very dooryard."

"So far as that?" said Alfred.

"Yes," resumed Nepsey, while she put the corner of her apron to her eye; "that was when my husband was lost. It was nearly midnight then, and the light in the beacon had gone out. He was determined to go and relight it. I tried to make him stay with me, but go he would. He went out—he got to the beacon and fired the lamp, but he never came back again."

"But how was he lost?" asked the boy, who had become interested.

"He must have been swept away. I looked out of the window and saw him in the beacon after he had fired the great wicks, and then I saw him turn to come down. A few minutes afterwards the windows of this room were broken in with a loud crash, and I heard the great sea as it rolled over. My husband must have gone with it, for I never saw him afterwards."

Alfred arose from his seat and went to the side of the woman. She was sobbing beneath the smart of the wound she had opened, and the boy placed his arm about her neck, and tried to soothe her. He was successful, for Nepsey kissed the kind-hearted boy and smiled.

At nine o'clock, Alfred sought his bed, but he could not sleep. The wind howled so about the low walls, and the waves roared so upon the rocky shore, that he could only remember that fearful, dreadful night when he himself had been torn from the breaking ship, and washed up to where the light-keeper had found him. That was four years before, when he was only four years old, but the scene was as fresh and vivid before his mind as though he possessed the mental powers of manhood. He remembered nothing back of the storm save the face and blows of Marrok Pettrell, a man who had professed to be his father; but he could only think of Pettrell with horror. Upon Luke Garron he fastened his childish love. He had been born into the world of enjoyment when he first found shelter beneath the keeper's roof: he was the child of the storm, and Luke had often called him his little "Storm Child."

It was no wonder that Garron loved this Storm Child, for the little fellow was all goodness, all kindness, gratitude, and love. He remembered just enough of the first four years of his life to form a contrast with the present, and that contrast filled him with thanks and gratitude. His mind held a fear engendered by the visit of Pettrell, the preceding afternoon, but his young soul reposed with considerable confidence in the power of Garron. Both Garron and himself had thought Pettrell dead until the present time; they thought he had been lost at the time when Alfred was wrecked; but his appearance—Garron knew from Nepsey's description that it must be he—had dispelled the supposition.

It was after ten o'clock when Alfred fell asleep. At midnight he was awakened by the breaking in of his window. He leaped from his bed, and the first thought that flashed across his mind was of the sea's having reached the house; but it was only the wind, after all, that had blown the window in. He soon calmed his worst fears, but he could not think of retiring again. The wind was still howling with all its might, but the rain had nearly ceased falling. Occasional drops, however, came driving down like half-spent pistol-balls.

The boy sought the kitchen, and Nepsey was there over the fire. He asked for his father, and was told that he was in the beacon. The woman tried to persuade Alfred from venturing out, but it was of no avail. He drew on his coat, and having buttoned it closely about him, he put on his cap and left the house. For several moments after he had gained the yard, he was obliged to give way before the tempest. The wind came near taking him upon its bosom and bearing him off, but he at length braced himself and faced it, and after a long and tedious effort he reached the beacon. The door was on the leeward side of the structure, and he opened it and closed it after him without difficulty. He ascended the narrow stone stairs and found Garron seated near the lamps.

"Mercy on me! Why, what brought you here, Alfred?" exclaimed Luke, as the boy approached him.

"I came to seek you, father. Oh, how dreadfully it blows!"

"But you should not have ventured out, my child."

"I could not stay in my room, for the wind has blown one of my windows in. I had rather be here with you."

"Your room would have been safer than this place," returned Garron.

"Then what makes you stay here?"

"To see that the lamps do not go out. They have been out twice now. The wind draws through the crevices in the door, and sometimes it comes up here in gusts."

The beacon did vibrate beneath the power of the gale, and Alfred could not but feel a degree of alarm as he felt the returning shocks, but he soon became used to it, and a sense of novelty overcame his fear.

"This is dreadful, and yet how grand it is," uttered the boy, as he crept down by the side of his guardian. "If it wasn't for the danger of life to these poor folks at sea, I could almost wish this would last. It makes me feel like a man to face up such a storm."

Garron gazed on the upturned face of the boy, and a smile lit up his features. But the smile soon passed away, and with a sober look he laid his hand upon Alfred's head.

"You feel safe, my child, because I am here with you," he said.

The boy silently acknowledged the truth of the remark.

"You say you feel like a man," continued Garron, with a tone of deep pathos and meaning. "You feel like a man because you can face this storm and brave all its dangers; but when you grow up to be a man in years, do you think you can face all the storms you may meet?"

Alfred looked inquisitively at his guardian.

"You will then have other storms to face. Perhaps in a few years you will be cast upon the world, and be obliged to guide your own bark. Did you know there are such things as sin and wickedness in the world?"

"Yes," said the boy, with a shudder.

"And did you know that evil men sometimes tempt the unwary into sin? Ah! my child, if you live to be a man, you will find many a storm of life to be faced, and he is a noble man who comes out safely from them all. When you came out of the house to-night, did you not have to stand still a few moments ere you could gain strength to make your way against the storm?"

"Yes; and it even took me back a little ways."

"Would it not have been very easy for you to have turned about and walked the other way?"

"Oh yes!"

"And why did you not do it?"

"Why, I should certainly have been lost."

"Yes. And why did you face the storm and walk bravely against it?"

"Why, because the beacon was this way."

"That's it, my child," returned Garron, as he drew the boy closer to him. "Now can you not always bear this simple thing in mind? You wish to be a good man when you grow up, and you wish to have your name honored?"

"Yes," said the boy.

"Then," resumed Garron, "let that be your beacon, and remember that to reach that beacon is the object of your journey of life. Let the wind be high or low, let it blow a tempest or a gentle breeze, keep your face towards the beacon, and push boldly forward. If the gale be against you, face it without fear. It may at times seem more easy to walk the other way when the tempest howls in your face, but remember that the ocean of danger may swallow you. Face about, brave the storm, and push on for your beacon. Think you can remember this?"

The boy arose to his feet, and after gazing for a moment into his protector's face, he threw his arm about the good man's neck, and gently murmured:—

"I shall never forget it."

The tempest howled, and the beacon trembled, but for a while the man and boy noticed it not. They were busy with other thoughts.

"Great God! what was that?" cried the light-keeper, lifting the boy from his knees and springing to his feet.

"I heard nothing but the wind," said the boy.

"No, no, 'twas not the wind. Ha! Did you hear that, Alfred?"

"I heard something. It was the break of a big wave on the rocks."

"Oh, no, it was a gun!"

"A gun!" repeated Alfred. "Then there must be some ship on the coast."

"Yes. Ah, there goes another. Stay you here. I will go down and see if I can make out her whereabouts. Another—and another. Oh, this is fearful!"

"I must go with you," said the boy.

"You had better stay."

"No, let me go. I can face the storm."

"Then come."

Luke Garron saw that the beacon lamps were all safe, and then he turned to descend the stone stairs. When he reached the ground he passed out, closed the door safely behind him, and then gave his hand to the boy. It was only a few rods to the head of the bluff, and with careful steps the keeper made his way along. The heavens were as black as ink, and the earth was buried in darkness; but the lashing waters of the broad Channel were visible in their phosphorescent glimmering, and the two companions could see the great white heaps of foam that came crashing upon the rocks.

They had to grope their way along with the utmost care, for a single false step would be dangerous. Alfred, however, bore bravely up, and Garron found that his help was not necessary to keep the boy up. He still held him by the hand, though, for he did not care to run the risk of danger. Ere long there came a dull boom upon the tempest, and Garron stopped. Another and another report followed in rapid succession.

"Those were guns, certainly," said Luke.

"Ah, then I saw a glimmer," said the boy.

Hardly were the words out of his mouth before the sound of the distant gun came rolling along. Alfred made his guardian understand the direction in which he had seen the glimmer, and it was soon seen again, and again the report followed.

"That is the spot," said the keeper, fastening his eyes upon the point in which he had seen the light.

"How far off is she?" asked the boy at the top of his voice.

"Not over six or seven miles," returned Garron.

"And the wind must be setting her this way," added the boy, bracing himself more firmly against the gale.

"Yes, yes," uttered the light-keeper, in a deep, heavy tone. "She is lost, lost!"

"If she don't work off," said the boy.

"Work off!" echoed Garron. "A piece of canvas no bigger than a hat-cover wouldn't stand before this gale. Work off! Would to God she could, for Heaven knows I can give her no aid! I can only look up the ill-fated crew in the morning."

It was now near two o'clock in the morning. The rain had ceased falling altogether, and away off in the western heavens there appeared to be a breaking in the black sky. Still the light-keeper and the boy stood upon the bluff and gazed off to where ever and anon appeared the lightning of the ship's guns. Those guns still boomed over the waters, but the tempest mocked at them, and howled down their terror-laden notes.

The ill-fated ship had now been driven so near that the report followed closely upon the flash of the gun. It was evident to Garron that she would strike before she could reach the bluff. She seemed driving towards a point about half a mile to the westward of the spot where the watchers stood, and would thus strike the extreme western sweep of the promontory.

"The people at Comb Martin may have heard the guns, and some of them may come out," said the boy.

"Perhaps so; but that is sixteen miles from here, and no one would be very likely to follow the ship," returned Garron. Oh! God knows I cannot ward off the blow! They are in the hands of One who doeth all things well, and he will have called many a soul home to himself ere another sun shall rise. God have mercy on them, and I will do what I can."

For a long time the two watchers stood in silence. The ship came nearer and nearer. It was now evident that she would strike, as Garron had anticipated. The break in the western sky had grown larger, and the heavy edges of the black clouds could be seen as they began to break away from the bosom of the Atlantic and roll up into the heavens. The gale seemed to slacken. Perhaps it was because the watchers had become inured to it. Yet its fury was on the wane.

"I think I can see her," uttered the boy, pointing with his hand towards the spot where it had been thought the ship would strike.

The light-keeper looked, and he could just distinguish a black mass upon the surging waves. His hands were clasped in fearful suspense.

"Did you see her?" asked the boy.

"Yes, Alfred."

"Oh, how near she is! Look! Look!"

"Her last moment is at hand!" murmured Luke Garron, as he bent his head forward and strained his eyes towards the fatal scene.

"Hark!" shudderingly uttered the boy.

At that moment there came a wild, fearful cry over the lashing surge. Then came a crashing—a rumbling of rending timbers—and again that wild cry broke upon the tempest.

CHAPTER III.

THE WRECK, AND THE STORM CHILD.

THE first gray streaks of morning were in the east. The tempest had passed over in its fury, but the wind murmured a mournful requiem, and the great heavy waves rolled sluggishly in from the ocean. Luke Garron armed himself with a short hook and a hatchet, and a coil of light rope, and with Alfred for a companion, he set forth towards the scene of the wreck.

As they descended the bluff towards the west they could just distinguish the outlines of the ragged mass of timbers that were fastened among the rocks. When they reached the low shore they found that fragments of the wreck were lodged all along in the crevices of the low breakers, and the sea was breaking over them in wild confusion. At the distance of ten rods from the promontory the two companions suddenly stopped. Upon a small bed of gray sand, where the water washed in between two large rocks, lay the form of a human being. It was a seaman, and his face was turned downward. Luke turned the corpse over. The features were stiff and rigid.

"This is the beginning," murmured the light-keeper, as he brushed the sand from the cold face.

The boy did not speak, but he helped his protector draw the body further up on the shore, and then they passed on.

Ere long another body was found, and having drawn it up out of the reach of the sea, the companions set forward again; but they were soon stopped by a sight that chilled their blood. Three female forms lay close between two rocks, and they were clasped firmly in each other's embrace. Luke Garron stood for a moment without the power to speak.

"Oh!" uttered the boy, shrinking more

closely to his guardian, "this is dreadful. Think they are dead?"

"Yes," mournfully returned Luke. "They no longer know what it is to suffer. The voice of the storm is hushed to their ears, and they feel not the chill of the cold sea. Death is but death. The angel unlocks the doors of the soul and lets the spirit forth; yet it seems hard to have the spirit torn out thus."

Luke could not move the bodies of the women without help, and he moved forward. At length he reached the spot where the ship had struck. Great spars and timbers were strewed about over the beach and among the rocks. For the distance of many rods the sea was flanked with big rocks and sharp crags, while back towards the shore was spread a low beach. Most of the lighter stuff that had broken loose from the wreck was spread upon this beach, but the heavy parts were lodged among the rocks. The ship had struck her bows upon the breakers, and had then been literally knocked to pieces. For a long time Luke Garron searched for some living witness who might tell to him the story of the ship and her crew, but not one could he find. There were witnesses enough to tell the sad story of the wreck, and of its load of death, but they were all silent—their lips were sealed.

Many of those who had thus met their death, Luke knew must have been passengers. From the bales and boxes which were scattered about him, he knew that the ship had been an Indiaman. For nearly an hour the light-keeper continued his search, but every face he met was stiff and cold.

The boy had been walking alone. His soul was filled with awe, and with a fearfully beating heart he gazed upon the ghastly emblems of mortality that lay about him. While his companion was hunting among the rocks, Alfred walked back to the spot where the three females were lodged between the rocks. He reached the place, and for a long time he stood still and gazed upon the scene. Perhaps he was thinking of one who might have been his own mother; one whom he fancied he could remember, but whom he could only see in his young heart's affection, for his memory retained no image of the loved ideal.

Suddenly the boy started, for he thought he heard a sound issue from one of the women, and he was sure that he saw a movement of the drapery that clung about the cold forms. He sprang forward and laid his hand upon the brow of her who laid uppermost, but there was no life there. The other two faces he could see, and he was sure that no life animated them. The sea broke over the spot, and all drenched with water the boy made his way to the sand. "It was only the gurgling of the water among the rocks," he said to himself, as he turned his eyes again upon the scene.

But again he heard the sound, and he saw the drapery move. Once more he sprang forth upon the rocks and knelt down by the side of the corpse. Again he heard the sound that had startled him, and one of the dresses moved beneath his hand. It was surely the voice of a child he heard!

With the strength that might have become a man, Alfred raised the uppermost form. His heart leaped with a wild thrill as he beheld a little child nestled away in the embrace of the female he had moved. It opened its eyes as the light came in upon it, and a sharp cry broke from its lips. It was a girl, and as the boy raised her in his arms she laid her little head upon his bosom and began to cry.

The child's resting-place had been so shielded from the sea, that its force had been lost upon her, and she had not been struck by any of the timbers or rocks. Two of the women seemed to have been clasped together so as to shield the child, while the third clung to her companions from the instinct of safety. Of course, the little thing was wet and cold, but it seemed not to have been bodily harmed.

With hasty steps the boy made his way back to the beach, and then cried out at the top of his voice for his guardian. Garron heard him, and hastened to the spot.

"Oh, see, see!" cried Alfred; "I have found a living child."

"God be thanked!" uttered Luke, as he took the child in his arms and gazed into its face. "One life, at least, is saved to earth. The little thing is cold. We must hasten to the house with it, and then come back again."

"Let me carry her," cried the boy.

"You are not strong enough, Alfred. It would take you too long, and she is very cold now,"

Luke strode on towards his house with the child, and Alfred ran along by his side.

"Here, Nepsey," said Garron, as he entered the kitchen, "here is a charge for you. Get something dry for it as soon as possible."

"But its mother—where is she?" asked the old woman, as she took the child in her arms, and instinctively kissed it.

"I'm afraid this child is the only one saved from the wreck. We can find no more of life."

"No more! All gone!" ejaculated Nepsey.

"Yes, all gone! But hurry and make the most of this."

The woman was for some moments deprived of her reasoning faculties, but at length she gathered her senses together, and kissing the child again, she turned towards the fire.

"Another child of the storm," she said, as she fixed a seat for her charge.

The light-keeper gazed thoughtfully upon the child, and a kind look—almost a smile—broke over his features.

"It is the second of my STORM CHILDREN," he said. "Be careful of her, Nepsey."

There was no need of this charge, for the woman was hurrying to fix a warm, dry dress, and the cast of her countenance showed that her heart was enlisted in the work.

Luke Garron started to return to the scene of the wreck, and Alfred followed him. When they again reached the spot, they found that a number of men had arrived from Comb Martin, and in less than an hour over an hundred people had assembled about the place. The bodies were all collected—or at least, such as could be found, and before noon two of the coroners of Devonshire, with other officers, were upon the spot. The ship was found to be the "Chesham," but none of her papers could be found. At the request of Garron the bodies of the three females were carried up to his house, and the others were placed in wagons and carried to Comb Martin.

The proper officers took charge of the wreck, and their men set about the work of collecting such things as were of value. The deep waters of the bay were settling into quiet once more. They seemed like the fatigued lion who has performed his work of death, and goes crouching away to his rest.

It was nearly night when Luke Garron returned to his house. The child was asleep, and he sought his own bed to gain, if possible, a little rest before it would be time to light the beacon. Alfred, too, was tired, and he early sought that sleep of which he had been deprived the preceding night.

The next morning was bright, and the little girl who had been saved from the wreck was running about the kitchen calling for her "mama." She was a bright-eyed creature, about four years old, and her hair hung down upon her shoulders in glossy ringlets. Her cheeks were wet with tears, nor could Nepsey comfort her. The light-keeper took her in his arms and carried her to where the bodies of the three females had been laid.

"Mama, mama!" cried the child, reaching forth her little hands towards the female from whose embrace Alfred had released her.

"Is that mama?" asked Garron, laying his hand upon the cold brow of the woman in question.

"Yes, my mama—my mama!" cried the child, struggling to get away from the man who held her.

"I think not," returned Luke. "That woman is certainly Scotch, and there is no likeness between her and the child."

"But the child must know its own mother," said Nepsey; but she spoke in a doubting mood, for she saw the disparity which Luke had pointed out. The woman was Scotch in dress and feature, and not far from forty years of age.

"It may be only a nurse," said Garron. "It certainly cannot be a mother. If she is the nurse who has always had charge of the child, she would naturally call her 'mama.'" The child still cried for its mama, and Garron at length carried her away. Alfred took her, and with the boy she soon became composed. She laughed with him, and before the day was passed she had learned to regard him with manifest affection. She seemed to regard him with more favor than she did the older people, though she still had spells of crying for her "mama." She said her name was Ella Dean.

At the end of a week from the time of the wreck, Ella had become quite satisfied with her new home. She laughed and played with Alfred, smiled when Luke took her in his arms, and called Nepsey her "mama." Word had been sent out of the circumstance, but no one came to claim the little girl, and the light-keeper began to look upon her as his own. Her bright presence called new smiles to his face, and with Alfred upon one knee, and Ella upon the other, he loved to sit and laugh and play with his Storm Children.

CHAPTER IV.

A STRANGE TRANSACTION.

BACK of the beacon house, beneath the shade of the great oak, Luke Garron had made three graves, and within their silent chambers he deposited the remains of the females who had been brought to his house. He could find no clew to their names, and he simply raised a slab upon the spot, which bore upon its surface a simple record of the event that had transpired. He was firm in his conviction that neither of the women could have been the mother of Ella, for the child seemed to recognize only one of them, and all the rules of physiognomy set aside the supposition that that one could have been any kin to the girl.

Two weeks had passed away, and Ella Dean was happy. She piped forth her joyous notes like a warbling bird, and with Alfred by her side, she was happy. Sometimes she spoke of her "other mama," and tears would start to her eyes, and her little lips would tremble; but a kiss from Alfred would dispel the cloud and light up her face with smiles again.

It was just after noon, on a pleasant day, and the two children were at play before the house. Luke Garron had gone down to his boat, and Nepsey was about her work in the building. Suddenly Alfred was startled by the appearance of three men who had come up through the path from the woods. One of them he recognized as the man who had been there two weeks before, and he was sadly frightened.

Marrok Pettrell—for it was he—gazed a few moments on the boy, and then he went up to where he stood.

"Your name is Alfred?" said Pettrell.

"Yes, sir."

"Alfred Pettrell?" continued the man.

"No, no—Alfred Harrold," uttered the boy, trembling with fear.

"No. Your name is Pettrell. You are my own son. Don't you remember me? Don't you remember when we were cast away together?"

"Oh, no, no! I don't remember you!" cried the boy moving back with terror. "Good Luke Garron is my father."

"I declare," said one of Pettrell's companions, with a coarse laugh, "the boy doesn't know his own father. Well, blow me if that aint a rum go!"

"It can't be expected, Bronkon," returned Pettrell, "for I haint seen the boy before for four years. But come, my son," he continued, turning toward Alfred, "you will go with me, now."

"No, no!" exclaimed the boy. "I wont go with you. I'll go and find my father."

Alfred started to run away as he spoke, but the man caught him by the arm.

"Stop, stop, my boy. I am your father, and I have come to take you."

Alfred cried with terror, and little Ella screamed and started towards the house. Nepsey came out to see what was the matter, and at that same moment Luke Garron came up from his boat.

"Father, father!" cried Alfred, breaking

away from Pettrell and running to the light-keeper, "you wont let these ugly men take me away?"

Luke seemed to recognize Marrok Pettrell at once, for his face turned pale, and he trembled.

"Your name is Garron, I take it?" said Pettrell, advancing towards Luke.

"Yes," returned the light-keeper, laying his hand upon the shoulder of the shrinking boy.

"Then I've come to get my son. That's him."

"Your son!" repeated Garron.

"Yes. That youngster who seems to take such a fancy for you. He's my child—my own blood, and I want him."

"You cannot have him," firmly returned Luke.

Marrok Pettrell laughed.

"That is a go!" said Bronkon.

"A queer business," added Pettrell, "for a father to be denied his own child."

"He is not your child," said Luke.

"No; I am your own child—your own boy!" cried Alfred.

"Now you make me out a liar!" said Pettrell. "Was not that boy thrown upon the coast here four years ago this spring?"

"Yes," answered Luke, after a moment's hesitation.

"Of course he was; and it was my own vessel that was wrecked," resumed Pettrell. "I was washed ashore about six miles beyond Porlock on a spare spar. I always thought my boy was lost till about a month ago, and then I heard that you had found him. Of course I knew it was my boy. Now I want him."

Luke Garron trembled like an aspen, and he knew not what to do. The boy clung to him, and begged for his protection.

"You cannot—must not take him," uttered Garron, in despairing accents.

"What; not have my own flesh and blood?" exclaimed Pettrell, with much surprise.

"I do not believe"——

"Blow your belief," impatiently interrupted Pettrell. "I want my boy, and that is enough for an honest man. Hope you do not want me to use force?"

The light-keeper doubled up his fists as he heard these words, and the muscles of his arms worked like big cords. The quick flush of anger, however, passed from his face, and he bore a look of the keenest anguish.

"Let me keep him," he said. "In God's name I implore you let me keep him. He has become part of my very life, and I cannot part with him."

"I'm really sorry to give you so much pain," coolly replied Pettrell; "but what is mine is mine, and I must have it; so the boy must come along."

Garron stood and held the boy, but he had lost his firmness. Dark clouds passed over his features, and once his hand rested upon the pistol in his belt.

"Come, Pettrell, take the boy, and let's be off," said Bronkon.

Marrok Pettrell moved towards the place where the boy stood.

"Keep back!" gasped Luke. "Lay not a hand upon him! He is my child!"

"Your child!" laughed Pettrell, in derision.

"Mine by right of justice," continued Luke. "I saved him from the cold sea, and I have nursed and reared him from a little child. He's mine! mine!"

"Not quite, so stop your foolery, and give me my boy."

Pettrell caught Alfred by the arm as he spoke, and pulled him away from the light-keeper.

"Save me! save me! Oh, for God's sake save me!" cried Alfred.

Little Ella shrieked and ran into the house.

In a moment all Luke's firmness returned to him. The cries of the loved boy overcame all other emotions but those of love for the child, and with one blow of his powerful fist he knocked Marrok Pettrell over on the greensward, and then seized the child in his arms. He had commenced a contest, however, which he could not carry out, for both the other men sprang upon him, and a blow from the butt of Bronkon's pistol laid him senseless upon the ground.

When Luke Garron came to himself, old Nepsey was bending over him, and little Ella was kneeling by his side.

"Where—where—is my boy?" were his first words, as he arose to his elbow.

"Gone! They've carried him off!" said the woman.

The light-keeper sprang to his feet and gazed wildly about him.

At that moment a body of horsemen, at the head of whom was the sheriff of Somerset, came galloping towards the house.

"Have there been three men — three strangers—near here?" hastily asked the sheriff, as he pulled up his horse by the side of Luke.

"Yes, yes," quickly returned Nepsey, while her master was collecting his senses.

"And where are they now?"

"Gone off into the woods. Off that way," said the woman, pointing towards the path that led out into the Porlock road.

"How long since?"

"Not over fifteen minutes."

"Hold!" exclaimed Luke, as the sheriff was turning away; "who is it you seek?"

"A fellow named Pettrell, and two of his men. They are smugglers."

Oh, sir, bring me back the boy they have with them. They have stolen him away from me."

"The boy I have seen here with you?"

"Yes—yes."

"You shall have him if I can but find the rascals."

As the officer spoke he turned his horse's head toward the wood, and his men followed him.

Nepsey explained to her master how the men had seized Alfred and borne him off, and how he cried for help. The stout man shook as he heard the story, and he groaned with bitter anguish. Little Ella cried and talked about the "ugly old men" till she had worried herself to sleep in Nepsey's lap.

Till long after nightfall did Luke Garron sit upon a rock at the corner of his house and strain his aching eyes off towards the woods, and it was not until the darkness had fairly set in that he thought of the beacon. When he did think of his neglected duty, he moved very slowly to its performance, and heavy sighs escaped from his lips. After he had lighted the lamps in the beacon, he came down and proceeded to the house.

"Garron," said Nepsey, after she had regarded the anguish-wrought features of her master for some time in silence, "do you think that man is the father of Alfred?"

"No," returned Luke, with a sudden start.

"Then what does all this mean?"

"Mean?" repeated Luke.

"Yes."

"You see as well as I do."

"Then you have no idea of why that man wishes to take the boy away?"

The light-keeper looked up into Nepsey's face, and a shudder ran through his frame.

"Don't you think you have as much right to the boy as this Pettrell has?" continued the woman.

Luke remained silent.

"Tell me, Mr. Garron," persisted she, "have you not as much right to Alfred as Pettrell has?"

"You know I found the boy, and saved his life," at length returned Luke; "and that surely gives me good claim until another is presented stronger. The ties of blood would outweigh the mere saving of life."

"But you don't believe there is any tie of blood between Pettrell and the boy?"

"Tie of *blood!*" uttered the light-keeper, while he trembled more fearfully than before.

"Between Pettrell and the boy," added the woman, not seeming to notice the effect produced upon her master.

"No, no, there can be none—none that I know."

"Then make Pettrell prove his right to the boy."

"It's too late now."

"No. He will come back. I know the officers will overtake those men."

"Do you think he will come back?" asked Luke.

Nepsey started at the strange tone of Garron's voice—it was so different from its usual strong and open volume. And then his mind, too, seemed to be so wandering, just as though he could not govern his thoughts.

"I know he will come back," she answered. "The men cannot turn from the path till they reach the road, and the officers will overtake them before that. I'm sure Alfred will come back."

"God send it."

"And now if he does come," resumed the woman, "you won't let him go again? Make Pettrell prove his right first. Oh, it is dreadful to think of how the poor little fellow must suffer. If I had been a man he should never have gone as it was."

"If Pettrell is taken and convicted of smuggling, he may be hanged!" exclaimed Luke, half starting from his chair.

"Perhaps so," said Nepsey.

"Then he will never come again for the boy."

Nepsey was certainly puzzled by the manner of her master, and she showed it plainly in her looks. She did not have an opportunity to speak, however, for at that moment the sound of a horse's hoofs was heard coming around the house. Luke sprang to his feet and rushed to the door, where he arrived just in season to see his boy sliding down from behind an officer. He caught the lad in his arms and lifted him to his bosom.

"Did you catch the men?" he asked of the rider.

"No; but the others are after them. We pressed them hotly, and they dropped the boy and took to the woods, so the sheriff sent me back with him. He's safe and sound, sir."

The man rode off, and Luke returned into the house. Alfred was shaking with the effects of his fear, but he soon grew calm; and then he related to his protector how the men had carried him off—how the officers came near overtaking them, and how they dropped him.

"Oh!" he uttered, "that man is not my father. I will never live with him. I would run away and come back to you, for I love you."

"Bless you, my boy, bless you!" ejaculated Garron, as he folded the boy to his bosom. "The officers may take the wicked man, and then he will trouble us no more."

"I hope they will take him," said Alfred, "for Pettrell told me when he set me down in the woods, that he would have me if he had to die for it. He said I was his child."

Luke tried to assure the boy that he was safe, and at length the little fellow sought his bed. Garron remained in the house until nine o'clock, and then he went to see the light.

The keeper stopped as he reached the yard in front of his house, and looked about him. The stars were glittering like tiny lamps in the heavens, and the breeze came in cool and refreshing from the broad Atlantic. The sea was capped by long, low swells, that broke mournfully upon the rocks; and after gazing for some time upon the dark bosom of the channel, Luke Garron moved slowly towards the beacon. His steps were heavy, and he seemed sad at heart.

CHAPTER V.

A TERRIBLE BLOW.

WE must now pass over eight years. In handling events of the past, such a step is easily taken, and though we fly, Parnassus-like over the gulf, yet we cannot hide the marks of change, nor the indelible foot-prints of old Time. Eight years! How simple the expression; and yet how important may have been the epoch. Kingdoms have been built in eight years, and in the same time great nations have fallen. In eight years what hosts of humanity have been swept away from the earth, and what countless numbers of beings have started fresh and strong in the race of life. Great hopes have ended in fruition, and greater hopes have been crushed. Many a flower has withered and died, and many a blossom has opened its leaves to the warm sun, in all the joyousness of sweet and happy life. Eight years have passed. Some men have grown better,

—some have grown worse—and some stand like cold lumps of unimpressible granite, in the same spot upon the moral road; and there they will stand till a hand more powerful than the love of gain, shall snatch them away from a world that shall never miss them.

Time has passed; yet the same immutable laws govern God's world of humanity. Sin has the same fitful glare, to dazzle the eyes of the fool, the same deep-laid snares for the unwary, and the same sharp thorns for its victims. Calm Virtue still holds in her hand the same lustrous lamp of holy flame, which no gale or storm can extinguish; her face still bears the same sweet smile, and her followers are still happy.

With Luke Garron time had made but little change. A few gray hairs have set themselves upon his head, and a few wrinkles have been marked upon his countenance; but he still bears the same noble, generous look, and his black eye is undimmed. With the Storm Children the change has been great. Alfred Harrold has grown to be a large boy, for he has just seen his sixteenth birthday. He is tall for his age, and his form has been developed in manly beauty. His hair is still glossy in its hue of light brown, and his eye is still light in its liquid blue. The very thought-marks upon his fair countenance show that he has studied to some purpose, beneath the teachings of his generous protector.

And little Ella, now smiling in her twelfth year. Oh, how beautiful, how lovely, and how happy! Her dark brown hair floats in glittering ringlets, and from out the depths of her soft, hazel eyes there shines the light of her whole affectionate heart. She walks where Alfred walks; she sits where Alfred sits; she reads in Alfred's books, and Alfred teaches her the same lessons he has been taught. When Alfred smiles upon her, she throws her little white arms about his neck and kisses him; and then they talk of love; such love as hearts feel that know nothing beyond the world of purity and peace.

Nepsey's step has grown slower and weaker, but she has help from the children, and she loves to hear them laughing and talking about her.

It was towards night on a day of early autumn. Luke and Alfred stood upon the bluff that overlooked the small cove. Ella had just gone into the house, for the evening air was becoming damp and cool.

"She's a fine sailer," said Luke. "See how she slips along through the water."

The light-keeper alluded to a brig that was coming up the Channel, and at which he and Alfred had been looking.

"She is, indeed, a pretty craft," returned the youth. "Let me take the glass a moment."

Luke handed him the spy-glass, and he raised it to his eye.

"She has no ports, but I think I can see guns upon her deck," he said.

"Guns!" uttered Luke. "You must be mistaken. Let me look."

Luke took the glass.

"No," he resumed, after he had looked a few moments; "those are not guns. They are water-casks."

"But what do you make her out to be?" asked Alfred. "She does not look like a government vessel, nor does she look like a trader."

"She may be one of those Yankee traders bound up to Bristol," said Luke, still looking through his glass.

"But she's got no load," suggested the youth.

"She may have come from Brest. Ah, what's that? She's luffing, as sure as the world."

The wind was southwest, and the brig had been leaving it upon her starboard quarter; but as the old man spoke, she had put her helm down, and was hauling in her lee braces —and her head was consequently coming about towards the promontory.

"What can she want here?" Luke continued.

"It may be a smuggler, who thinks to land his goods above here," said Alfred.

At the mention of that word, Luke Garron trembled. Alfred noticed it, and he looked earnestly into the old man's face.

Again Luke levelled his glass; but the deepening shades of evening dimmed the view, and he could see the brig's deck but indistinctly.

"She's entirely in the wind now," said Alfred.

"Yes; and there goes her anchor."

The two watchers could see the brig's sails were being clewed up, and that her yards were braced to the wind. It became too dark to see more, and the light-keeper turned towards the house, whither Alfred followed him. Soon afterwards the great lamps were lighted in the beacon, and then Luke repaired to the sitting-room. At eight o'clock Ella went to bed; but a strange fear had seized upon the mind of Alfred, and he could not think of sleep. He did not think of sliding off into the woods, but he tried to quell the rising alarm by endeavoring to persuade himself that all was safe.

It was nine o'clock, and Luke had just arisen for the purpose of going to look after the beacon light, when he was startled by the sound of footsteps and voices in front of the house. A moment afterwards there came a knocking upon the door, and Nepsey went to see who was there.

Luke Garron sank back into a chair, and Alfred sprang to his side, as Marrok Pettrell entered the room! He was followed by four men, two of whom were the same that attended him eight years ago.

"A pleasant evening to you," said the smuggler.

Luke did not speak.

"Can't ye welcome an old friend?" continued Pettrell.

"Do not profane that sacred name," said Garron, clutching his hands in nervous anxiety; "but tell me what you seek?"

"I've come to seek what I lost eight years ago," returned Pettrell, casting a peculiar look upon Alfred.

"You mean the boy?"

"Yes."

"Then you can go as you went then."

"Without him?"

"Yes."

"No, no, Mr. Garron; I've come now to some purpose. The boy's grown to be a stout fellow, and he'll be of service to me. He's my own son, and have him I'm determined to."

"Marrok Pettrell"——

"Ah," interrupted the smuggler, "how do you know me so well?"

Garron changed color; but he soon overcame the emotion, and returned:—

"I've heard your name from the revenue officers."

"Ah! Then you have heard my name used rather lightly. But it's the fate of honest men to be maligned. Come, Master Alfred, you must ship under your father's flag for the future."

"Not under yours!" returned the boy.

"There's spunk," said Bronkon, with his usual coarse laugh.

"Ay, and I shall like him the better for it," added Pettrell.

"You cannot have the lad," said Luke Garrou, who had assumed a fearless look, and arisen from his chair. "You know that he is not your child, and that you have no earthly right to him."

"Avast a bit, Mr. Garron. Where did you get the boy?"

"I saved him from the wreck of a vessel years ago."

"Yes, and he was my child, and I lost him. Great guns and thunder! do you think yourself the owner of everything you find? I'm really obliged to you for the care you've taken of the youngster, and perhaps I'll pay you sometime; but for the present I think I'll take my property to my own keeping. So come along, Master Alfred!"

"Never!" said the youth.

"That's good," contemptuously returned the smuggler; and then, while a darker shade settled upon his features, he added:—

"But mark ye, my boy—not having had you under my protection, perhaps I might not be so tender of ye as you've been used to. You'll find it pleasant sailing if you keep your sails trimmed right; but if you are going to lay your canvass aback, you'd better look out for squalls. Do you understand that?"

Alfred was bold, and his heart was strong in moral right, but he had been tenderly reared, and he shuddered as he met the gaze of Pettrell, and heard his portentous words.

"I don't s'pose there's any need of more talk," resumed the smuggler, as he moved towards Alfred. "I have come after my boy, and I don't think 'twill be for your good to make any resistance."

Luke Garron gazed upon the smuggler, and then he turned his eyes upon Alfred. His face had turned as pale as death, and he trembled at every joint.

"I will not leave you, father," cried the youth, throwing his arms about the old man's neck.

Garron started back and drew his pistol. It trembled a moment in his hand, and then he put it back again in his belt.

"Do not take him! Oh, do not!" he uttered, as he strained the boy to his bosom.

"Garron," said the smuggler, while his features softened in their expression, "you ask of me an impossibility. The boy is mine—I want him—and I must have him. Now there's no use in saying another word. You know there's no law on earth that would give you a right above my claim. I've got nothing against you. I forgive you for the blow you struck me eight years ago: but don't raise your hand to do such a thing again."

"I cannot—will not go!" exclaimed Alfred.

"You'll go with your father?" said the smuggler, coaxingly.

"Out upon you! you miserable, wretched, vile, mean, disgraceful, wicked vagabond!" cried old Nepsey, springing from her seat. "There isn't a drop of your blood in that boy's veins, you know there isn't!"

"What a Tartar!" exclaimed Bronkon.

"Tartar, or not Tartar, I'm an honest woman; and God knows you came villains from your cradles!"

Nepsey grasped the back of her chair; but she was old and weak, and she soon settled back into her chair.

"Alfred—my boy—my son," whispered Luke Garron, while the smuggler's attention was turned towards Nepsey. "I cannot save you now; you must go with Pettrell. But forget not my counsels—escape if you can, and come to me. I do not believe he is your father. Oh, what a blow is this! I have loved you, but fate is against me! Go, Alfred—go! God bless you now and ever! Do not speak to me; do not let me hear your voice again, for I cannot bear it!"

Deep sobs choked the old man's utterance, and he sank powerless into a chair. Big tears rolled down his cheeks, and his head was bowed. Alfred clung to him with frantic energy, but he found no language for the emotions of his soul.

"Come."

The boy started as he felt the hand of Pettrell laid upon his arm.

"Come, my boy."

Alfred looked up, and as he met the gaze of the smuggler he sank upon his knees. Two strong men lifted him up and bore him away, but Luke saw not the movement. It was well he did not, for he had already more misery heaped upon his heart than he could bear.

At length the outer door was closed, and the tramp of feet sank lower in the distance. The old man raised his head. He and Nepsey were alone.

"Is he gone?" he whispered.

"Yes," returned the woman.

Luke groaned, and covered his face with his hands. Shortly afterwards he went out and ascended to the beacon, and there he remained through the long night. Early in the morning Nepsey went to look after her master. She found him stretched across one of the stout oaken braces in the top of the beacon, in a deep sleep. It was not yet open daylight, but the great lamp had gone out, and the wicks were stiff and cold.

The woman aroused him and he started to his feet. He rubbed his eyes and gazed about him, and then he sank upon the oaken brace, and bowed his head upon his breast. Nepsey took him by the hand to lead him down. He arose, and with trembling steps he followed her.

Ella came forth to seek her playmate;

but she could not find him. Nepsey told her Alfred had gone.

"But he will come back. He will come to see his Ella," the girl cried. And she ran to the old man's side, and asked him if Alfred would not come back.

For the sake of that sweet girl, the light-keeper kept back his heavy grief; but he could not wholly deceive her. She feared that Alfred would not come back, and she cried with an aching heart.

Pen cannot paint such sorrow as had fallen upon the old man and that bright-eyed child. Only the human heart can bear its impress; and to know it the heart must feel it.

When Luke walked out upon the bluff, the brig which had been there the night before had gone. No traces were left of her, save the pangs that dwelt with the memory of her presence, in his own bosom.

CHAPTER VI.

THE SMUGGLER.

ALFRED HARROLD (such was the name he had borne since he lived with Luke Garron, and so we call him) spoke not a word as he was being led down to the water. Once he struggled to free himself from the hold that was upon him; but the movement was in vain, and he tried it not a second time. When his conductors reached the cove, they put him on board a boat that was made fast there, and soon he was moving towards the brig. It was too dark when he passed over the gangway for him to distinguish objects about the deck, and he followed Pettrell down the after hatchway into the cabin. A hanging-lamp was burning there, and as the door closed behind them, Pettrell turned to the youth.

"Now," said he, "you are where you by right belong. I am master here, and my will is law. I am your parent, and I shall expect from you a child's obedience. If you choose not to give me that, however, I shall demand subjection of another sort. Can you understand?"

Alfred was silent. He gazed into the hard features of Marrok Pettrell, but he knew not what to reply.

"Will you not answer me?" sternly uttered the smuggler.

"I have no answer to make."

"I asked if you understood what I had said?"

Alfred Harrold had seen many storms—he had passed through many dangers, and more than once on the rough coast had he displayed a fearlessness that might have become a bold man. He had dared the heavy sea when men were in danger, and he had never shrank. His heart was strong now, and, as he gradually arose above the first stunning effects of the blow he had received, he felt a moral power that made him fearless.

"I have heard you speak," he said, "and I think I know what you mean."

"So far, so good," returned Pettrell, showing by his looks that he was a little surprised at the boy's lofty manner. "And how do you think you can obey me?"

"I can tell better when I know your commands."

"Ah! You are putting your foot on dangerous ground."

"I feel that, sir."

"Then you had better beware!"

"But it was you who brought me to the dangerous ground."

"You twist my meaning, youngster. I meant that your tongue was leading you into danger; so look out how you use it."

"I shall not be impudent, sir; but it is my right—a right given to me by God himself, through Christ, my Teacher—to maintain my integrity and my honor."

"P-h-e-w!" whistled Pettrell, with a look of contempt; but a close observer could have seen that his contempt was assumed. "You are bold for one of your years. But let me assure you of one thing: I stand your present talk with easy grace for me, but be careful that you don't show your independence before the men. It will be well for you to remember this. And now what do you know of sea matters?"

"Enough to sail a ship from here to Bristol."

"Ah. You will be useful, then. Is Luke Garron a seaman?"

"Few men know more of the sea."

"He has followed the sea, then?"

"He must have followed it at some time."

"Then I may thank him for teaching you seamanship, for such knowledge will be of much service to me. Your morality I advise you to keep for your own use."

The youth's eyes flashed, for the diabolical sneer of the man cut him to the soul.

"For the present," continued Pettrell, "you will take up your quarters in the cabin. I won't trust you in the forecastle yet. You can come on deck if you wish, but remember what I have said."

Pettrell turned and went on deck. For some minutes Alfred stood and gazed at the vacant spot where he had last seen the smuggler, and then his mind reverted to the terrible calamity that had befallen him. He staggered back and sank upon a low stool. It must have been full half an hour that the boy sat in one position and wept. He thought of his kind protector, and his soul was torn with anguish. He thought of Ella, and his heart sank into the burning depths of utter misery. He reflected that he might never again see those bright eyes—that he might never more behold that sweet face—that that beaming, happy smile would never again light his joy—and he groaned aloud. Then his thoughts dwelt upon the present—and then ran into the future, and he shuddered.

Then came back to his mind those words that Luke had whispered in his ear.

"He is not my father!" he uttered, while his hands were clasped in an agony of hope.

A strange expression, perhaps—but that boy did experience, at that moment, an *agony of hope!* He hoped the wicked man was not his father, and yet the hope was all agony.

At length Alfred started to his feet. He brushed the tears from his face, and then he clasped both his hands upon his heart.

"*Action!*" he murmured, as he turned his eyes towards heaven. "If this be God's will, then let it be done This is a fearful storm indeed; but I will face it while I have strength. Yes, my kind, generous protector, *I will not turn from the path that leads to the beacon!* God be with me, and guide me! There—I feel stronger now!"

A pure, a holy light shone upon the face of the boy as he now stood there in the smuggler's cabin, and he had fixed upon the course he would pursue. The details of that course he could not lay out, but he knew the object he had in view, and he only prayed for strength to sustain him in the endeavor. He felt the strength of a man in his soul, and his good muscles were strung for the trial.

When Alfred had so far regained his presence of mind as to turn his thoughts upon outward things, he found from the sound upon the deck that the men were heaving up the anchor. The atmosphere of the cabin seemed hot and oppressive to him, and he ascended the ladder. He could see the dusky forms of many men moving about the deck, and he could see the topsails were sheeted home and the yards mast-headed. The youth turned his gaze towards the shore; the dark outlines of the bluff were just visible, and beyond he saw the bright light of the beacon. He gazed upon the light for a moment, and then he bent his head and covered his face.

"Found the way on deck, eh?"

Alfred looked up and found Marrok Pettrell by his side.

"A free and jolly life is before you," continued the captain, "so you had better make up your mind to enjoy it."

The youth had no answer to return, and Pettrell turned his attention to the working of the brig. The anchor had broken ground, and the vessel was soon put upon the larboard tack and standing towards the coast of Wales. Alfred remained on deck half an hour, when he went back to the cabin. He crawled into the narrow berth that had been pointed out to him, and at length he slept.

It was broad daylight when Alfred awoke,

and again he passed through an ordeal of soul harrowing thought and reflection; but he knew that repining would never aid him, and uttering forth a simple prayer to God, he arranged his dress and went on deck.

The brig he found was a large one; and he found, too, that what he had taken for guns the night before, were, as Luke had said, nothing but water-casks. Yet he thought he could detect upon either side of the deck the marks of carriage wheels, and they ran at right angles with portions of the bulwarks that seemed made for moving in case of need. There were twenty-five men besides the captain on board. They were all stout fellows, and looked reckless enough for any calling that might turn up; yet some of them showed passing signs of respectable good nature in their countenances. Reckless they were, but not all so hard-hearted as the captain. There was one countenance, however, that seemed more repulsive than all the rest —and that was Bronkon's. He was a dark featured, powerful man, with a coarse, wicked expression of countenance, and he seemed to smile only when he saw misery about him. He was the second in command, and seemed a fit mate for the smuggler captain.

The morning was bright and clear; when Alfred reached the deck he found that the brig was just passing between Hartland Point and Lundy Island, with a fresh breeze from the eastward.

"Well, my boy, suppose I put you on one of the watches," said Pettrell, after he had allowed the youth sufficient time to look about him. "We don't have idlers here."

"You can do as you please," returned Alfred, conquering, with strong effort, his indignation.

"Then I shall put you in the starboard watch with myself. Your limbs show a pretty good quantity of muscle, and I think we'll show you how to use 'em. I tell you, Alfred, I think myself lucky in finding you."

"More lucky, probably, than I am in being found," returned the youth.

"That depends upon circumstances. You can make it lucky enough if you choose. Just let me give you a piece of advice: Learn to take the world just as you find it."

"That's the doctrine, youngster," said Bronkon, who stood near. "Take it as you find it, and make the most of it."

"I shall endeavor to get along the best way I can," answered Alfred. "My life so far has not been without its storms, and I have weathered them all. Of one thing you may rest assured; there is no fear of common danger hanging about my heart."

"Very good for a beginning," said Pettrell. "That's the right kind of a spirit, if you only use it in the right way. But we shall see."

As the captain turned away, Alfred reflected upon the course before him, and he was not long arriving at the determination to perform a seaman's duty to the best of his ability. He found himself placed in a position where he was not responsible for the business of the voyage, and from whence there was no present escape; so he knew no blame could attach to him so long as he laid not his hand to that which was really evil. He was most emphatically in a position where there were but two choices, and both of them evil. He chose that which offered the least evil.

CHAPTER VII.

THE BATTLE.

ALFRED HARROLD showed himself a good seaman, and though Pettrell seemed pleased with the manner in which he did his duty, yet he treated the youth with anything but kindness. He did not really abuse him, but his manner was unfeeling and coarse, and he was angry when Alfred refused to acknowledge him as a father. Among the men, however, the youth had made many friends. They could not but love one who was so kind and forbearing, though they were incapable of appreciating the moral feelings that gave source to the kindness they loved. Months passed away, and Alfred became more accustomed to his ocean home. The sharper points of his anguish were worn off; but his heart still turned with longing love towards the old light-keeper, and he dreamed sweet dreams, both sleeping and waking, of the bright-eyed Ella.

The brig went to Canton and took in part of a load of silks, and then touched at Sumatra and filled up with spices; and in nine months from the time of her leaving the Bristol Channel she was again upon the coast of England, and the season was summer. Alfred knew that the brig's cargo was to be smuggled on shore, and from remarks that he had heard, he knew that Pettrell had trusty agents in Lancashire.

The brig had entered the Irish Sea, and with a fresh breeze from the north-west was heading in towards the mouth of the river Ribble. It was near noon, when one of the men in the foretop reported a sail to the southeast. A consultation was held between Pettrell and Bronkon, and it was decided to stand on. The smuggler was now heading due east, and was not far from fifty miles from Lancashire coast.

"It may be only some trader coming out from Liverpool," said Bronkon.

"Very likely," returned the captain. And as he spoke, he levelled his glass upon the object of his consultation. "She's a schooner, I think," said he, as he lowered his glass and turned towards his mate.

"If it should be one of those infernal cutters," muttered Bronkon.

"She's heading this way," resumed Pettrell, again levelling his glass.

"Then she's a revenue hound, as sure as fate," said the mate. "Let me take the glass?"

Bronkon looked for several minutes, and when he lowered the glass a defiant smile broke over his coarse features.

"She's a revenue craft," he said. "I know her well, and shouldn't wonder if she knew us. We had better haul on the wind and lay up for Morecambe."

The captain assented to the proposal, and the brig's head was put up accordingly.

"We sha'n't get clear," muttered Pettrell. "She gains on us."

"If she must come, then let her come," returned Bronkon.

An hour passed, and the schooner was not two miles distant. Her guns could be seen peeping out from her sides, and it could also be seen that she carried a large number of men.

"This is going to be an ugly job," said the smuggler captain, pacing the deck with nervous strides.

"But we must make the best of it," coolly returned Bronkon.

"They won't take us without a blow, at all events," resumed Pettrell. "Waffon, get up the playthings."

The man who was thus addressed hurried below, and ere long he had brought pistols and cutlasses enough on deck for all the men, and the crew proceeded at once to arm themselves.

During this time Alfred had been a silent spectator of the scene. He saw that a fight with the schooner was inevitable, and his heart sank within him as he reflected upon the unfortunate position in which he was placed. He had hoped to reach the coast in safety, and there he determined to make good his escape, if possible; but this was a contingency he had not anticipated.

"Come, Alfred, arm yourself," said Pettrell. "We shall want your good arm in the coming conflict."

Alfred hesitated.

"You'd better," fell in low tones from Bronkon's lips.

A reply arose to Alfred's lips; but he suppressed it and went to the arm-chest. He took a cutlass and buckled its belt about his waist, and took a pair of the heavy pistols.

"There," said Pettrell, as he saw the youth armed, "now we will initiate you."

Just as the smuggler spoke there came a shot from the schooner, and passed through the mainsail.

"Rather a pressing invitation for us to heave to," said Bronkon.

"And I think I shall do it," said Pettrell. "There is no use in running any further. That schooner doesn't carry over forty men. We are twenty six—twenty-seven with Alfred—and I reckon we can give them a hard pull."

Another shot from the pursuing schooner, and in a few minutes afterwards the brig was hove to.

"Now let her come up," said the captain, as he looked around on his men. "Stand by, now, to take the first advantage, my boys. Remember that the enemy have the trouble of boarding. Have both pistols out for them the moment they show themselves over the rail."

Alfred seemed to have been forgotten in the excitement of the occasion. He stood near the larboard quarter rail, and he was gazing abstractedly upon the schooner, which was now almost alongside.

"Brig ahoy!" came from the revenue cruiser.

"What do you want?" returned Pettrell.

"I want you to surrender. Isn't that brig the 'Adder'?"

"Yes."

"Then I'll take you to Liverpool."

"Come and try it!"

"Do you mean to show fight?"

"Come and see!" was Pettrell's laconic reply.

The schooner was too near to use her guns, for she sat much lower in the water than did the brig, and she ranged up on the starboard side. Her men were ready for the leap, and the moment she touched they sprang for the smuggler's deck.

"Fire!" shouted Pettrell.

The smugglers poured in their volley on the boarders, and the effect was destructive. Eight of the schooner's men fell back upon their own deck, and for a few moments there was a suspension of further action. The schooner had now ranged fully alongside; again the revenue officer urged his men on.

"Fire!" shouted Pettrell.

Not over six of the boarders were knocked back by this fire, and the rest, to the number of twenty-seven, came rushing over the brig's bulwarks. The smugglers had fired their pistols, and they now had only their cutlasses upon which to depend, for they could not stop to reload. The boarders, on the other hand, had their pistols loaded, and they used them to good effect.

"Remember—the gallows if you are taken!" cried Bronkon, as he swung his heavy cutlass over his head and cut down a man who was before him. "At them, boys! Clear the 'Adder's' deck of the hounds!"

The smugglers fought desperately, and they had desperate foes to contend with. Pettrell was the commander, but Bronkon was the genius of the battle.

Alfred had not yet moved. The clang of the cutlasses rang with a deafening noise in his ears, and the fumes of gunpowder were hanging about him. While he stood thus, a great burly fellow rushed upon him.

"Ah, you smuggling son of a gun," yelled the assailant, "take that!"

It was a fierce blow that the big revenue man aimed at Alfred's head; but quick as thought the blow was dodged. With an instinctive movement the youth drew his own cutlass. His pistols were yet in his belt, and both of them were charged. Again the assailant swept his cutlass about his head, and his blow was coming down upon the youth. Alfred's brain whirled for a moment with its conflicting emotions; but the hope of life triumphed. That was not a moment to think of causes or consequences; he caught the eye of the stout man, and slipping quickly upon one side, he sank upon his knee and warded off the blow. The same movement of the cutlass that threw off the man's weapon brought the point up against his bosom, and with one powerful thrust Alfred laid his adversary upon the deck.

But he had no time to reflect upon what he had done, for at that moment Bronkon backed up against him with two of the revenue men driving at him. The smuggler mate was wounded upon the left arm, and there was a deep gash across his cheek, from which the blood was flowing copiously. He looked terrible in his gory features, but he was failing in strength. At the next blow he made, his cutlass was knocked from his grasp, and one of his assailants leaped upon him, and bent him back over the trunk of the cabin companion-way, while the other drove at him with his cutlass.

"God have mercy!" ejaculated Bronkon, in frantic tones; and as he spoke, his eyes rested upon Alfred.

There was a most imploring look in those rolling eyes, and Alfred could not withstand their silent appeal. It would have been fearful to see Bronkon killed as he then lay, and the youth entertained but a single thought as he dwelt upon the scene. His still reeking cutlass came down with a deadly blow upon the head of him who was about to strike, and with a pistol he shot the other through the temple. The act was more impulsive than premeditated; it was the silent look of appeal from Bronkon that influenced his soul, and whatever might be the result, he could not resist assistance in the man's hour of desperate need.

Bronkon arose to his feet, and gazed upon the face of the youth to whom he so signally owed his life.

"Alfred, I owe you one!" he said.

At that moment the boarders cried out for quarter, and the conflict stopped. Only twelve of the revenue men were alive to return to their schooner, and the majority of them were wounded. The brig had lost ten men, having sustained not half the loss of the other. Ere long the vessels were clear of each other, Pettrell having first, however, chopped the schooner's masts off near the deck, so that she could not run too soon with the news.

The dead were sewed up in hammocks and lowered over the side, the decks washed, and once more the brig turned her head towards the Ribble.

"Alfred," said Pettrell, "you behaved nobly."

The youth started from the painful reverie into which he had fallen, and gazed up into the face of the smuggler captain.

"Death and destruction!" uttered Bronkon, "but the youngster's arm served me most truly. I should have been food for sharks before now, but for him. Alfred, *I owe you one!*"

"You are worth more than I thought," added Pettrell. "Fore heaven, if you don't come on well!"

A dark shadow passed over the captain's face as he spoke, and a sort of demoniac triumph rested upon his features. Alfred Harrold turned away sick at heart. He shuddered at the thought of what he had done, but in his own soul he felt guiltless, and he knew that the blame must rest upon other shoulders than his. His earnest prayer was, that he might get clear of his present state of dreadful bondage.

CHAPTER VIII.

ESCAPE.—A STRANGE ACQUAINTANCE.

IT was nearly midnight when the brig's anchor dropped at the mouth of the Ribble, in a small cove near the outskirts of Kirkham, and as soon as her sails were clewed up, a blue light was hoisted at her foretruck, and a red one at her main. It was nearly three o'clock, however, before any notice was taken of these signals, but at that hour three large boats came alongside.

"You are a long while getting off," said Pettrell, to one of the men who came up from a boat.

"We didn't see the signals till an hour ago, and then we had to collect the men."

"How many have you got?"

"What—men?"

"Yes."

"There's eighteen of us."

"That will do; but we must hurry. I have only fifteen men left. We've had a brush with a revenue dog today, and it's thinned us down. Everything is ready ashore, isn't it?"

"Yes," returned the man from the shore, who was none other than the smuggler's agent, named John Pullen. The goods can be carried right to town. Three of the excise outriders are with us, so that coast is clear."

Most of the men were called up from the boats, a "yard and stay" whip-and-runner was rigged, and then all hands turned to at breaking out the cargo, which was hoisted into the boats alongside. The men worked smartly, and in less than five hours the whole cargo was safely landed on shore. Alfred watched in vain for an opportunity to get away from the brig, for as soon as she was clear she got up her anchor and made sail, Pettrell not daring to remain so near the scene of his late conflict. Arrangements were made with the agent, however, to meet the brig at a small rocky bay on the coast of Cumberland, some eight miles north of Whitehaven, and towards that place the smuggler made her way without being disturbed.

The wind had hauled around to the westward, and the brig reached her destination early in the evening, and shortly after the sails had been furled Pettrell went on shore; but before he went, however, he gave some whispered orders to his mate.

After the deck had been cleared up a quarter watch was set, Bronkon taking care that Alfred was stationed with himself. In each of these watches there were only three men, and they were merely set to keep a lookout for any boats that might come off, and also to look after the moorings.

The small bay in which the brig lay was not over a mile wide at the mouth, and where the smuggler was moored the distance from shore to shore was not over half a mile. She lay with her stern in towards the extremity of the bay, which was about a mile distant. On either shore were huge masses of rocks, with only an occasional break of sandy beach, while beyond the country was hilly and well covered with stunted oak. Not far from the head of the inlet, Alfred had noticed, as the brig first entered, a number of small houses, and towards these the captain had gone.

Pettrell had taken seven men with him in the boat, so that only nine were left on board, and Bronkon set them in three watches, with two hours to each watch. His own watch came from ten to midnight, and with him were Waffon and Alfred. Only a few remarks passed between Bronkon and the youth during the two hours. The former seemed ill at ease in the presence of the lad who had saved his life, and the latter was busy with his own thoughts.

Midnight came and the watch was relieved. Alfred still bunked in the cabin, and thither he went, Bronkon and Waffon keeping him company. The youth turned into his berth, but it was not to sleep. He lay so that he could see the mate, and he at length became assured that that individual was watching him. He remembered the whisperings of the captain, and he doubted not that he himself had been the object of it, and that Bronkon had been instructed to have an eye to all his movements.

Waffon was soon asleep, but the mate still kept his eyes open, and ever anon Alfred could see their bright balls shining on him. At first the youth thought it might be the pain of Bronkon's wounds that made him thus wakeful; but then he knew those wounds had not kept him from his duty, and besides, he showed no signs of suffering. At length Alfred turned over in his bunk and gave a sleepy yawn, and ere long he began to breathe that long, heavy, sonorous breath peculiar to sound sleep. The ruse took, for ere many minutes there was a nestling in the mate's berth, as though his limbs were being composed for rest, and not long afterwards he began to snore.

Alfred turned carefully over in his bunk and looked forth. By the dim light of the hanging-lamp, one small wick of which was burning, he could see that Bronkon was asleep. He waited a moment, and then he slipped noiselessly from his berth. With quick, self-possessed movements he rolled his heavier clothing into a small bundle, and tied it up in a handkerchief, and then he crept to the cabin windows. They swung on hinges at the top, and opened outward by means of a lanyard rove through an eye above the frame.

The youth unhasped one of the windows and carefully hoisted it. There was a creaking of the hinge, and Bronkon moved in his bunk. Alfred still held the lanyard, and remained quiet, and again the mate settled into his undisturbed slumber.

The youth listened for a moment to hear if the watch were moving on deck and he had the satisfaction of hearing all three of them conversing in one of the gangways. He knew there was not a moment to be lost, and taking his bundle between his teeth, he crept stealthily out through the window, from which he could just reach the falls of the starboard davit. This had been left hanging when the captain's boat had been lowered, and from its lower block the youth could easily drop into the water without a noise. Upon the sill he waited a moment, but no one had been aroused; and with a fervent prayer upon his lips he reached forth till he could grasp the fall, and then he let his body swing off. There was a slight creeking of the davit sheeves, but no one was startled by the sound, and noiselessly he let himself down into the water.

For some minutes Alfred worked his way very slowly from the brig; but at length he took courage and struck boldly out for the southern shore of the inlet. It was too dark for those on board the brig to see him now, for Alfred could but distinguish the bare outlines of the vessel, and without more fear of detection, he swam on with all his strength. The distance was not great, and the brave fellow reached the shore in safety, happening luckily to come upon one of the sand bars that made out from between the rocks.

When he reached the rising ground he found it somewhat difficult to make his way through the shrubby wood; but having put on his outer clothing and drawing on his boots, he pushed on. He had some idea of the direction of Whitehaven road, for he knew that it was not over a mile from the head of the bay; so he took a south-easterly course, thinking to strike the highway at a safe distance from the houses he had seen near the shore.

For two hours Alfred pushed on through the intricate wood, and just as he was beginning to despair of finding the road, he espied an opening ahead. When he reached it, he found himself in the highway he was seeking. In half an hour more he reached the market town of Whitehaven—but he did not stop. None of the people were yet stirring, and he hastened on through the place, thinking that he would find some peasant's cot where he could rest and refresh himself.

When Alfred had fairly cleared from the town, the first red streaks of morning were rising in the east, and ere long daylight was dancing over the country. From the top of a small eminence the youth saw another large town before him, which could not have been over five miles from the one he had left. To the right, just west of the town, he saw the massive ruins of an old castle, lifting its ragged battlements against the sky, the ivy-bound towers of which were catching the first rays of the sun, while ahead he saw the banks of a murmuring river. He knew the town must be Egremont—that the river was Eden, and that the smugglers had secret agents in the place.

Through Egremont Alfred determined to make his way without stopping. It was nearly six o'clock when he reached the town, and it was half-past six when he had cleared its southern confines. He felt hungry and fatigued, but he dared not stop within the town. At eight o'clock he came to an inn—a small, out-of-the-way place, and here he stopped. He had some money with him—money which he had been collecting to serve him in case of need—so he had no need of suffering with want.

The landlord of the inn was not a type of landlords generally, for he was a thin, sallow-visaged man; but yet he appeared good-natured enough for all necessary business purposes. Alfred made known his wants, and a substantial breakfast was soon prepared for him. Just as he sat down he heard a rattling of wheels at the door, and upon looking out at the window, he saw a post chaise that had driven up.

"Young man," said the landlord, opening the door of the room in which our hero was eating, "you'll have to make room for a companion at the table, for a gentleman has just come as wants his breakfast in a great hurry."

Without stopping to receive Alfred's answer, the landlord introduced the stranger, and then went for more victuals.

The new-comer was a man some sixty

years of age, dressed in a garb of fine blue broadcloth, with heavy gold buttons. He wore a cap with a heavy gold band, and a superb sword was hanging from a silken belt about his waist. Alfred knew that the buttons bore the arms of the royal navy, but he was at a loss to make out the rank of the wearer.

"Beautiful morning," said the stranger, seeming raised to a communicative mood by the flavor of his coffee, which he sipped with evident relish.

"Very," returned Alfred, with composure.

The old gentleman ate a piece of buttered toast very slowly for a hungry man, and at intervals he looked inquisitively into Alfred's face.

"Are you from the north?" he asked, as he helped himself to a second slice of toast.

"Yes," returned Alfred, with some embarrassment.

Again the stranger looked into the youth's face more earnestly than before.

"Do you belong about here?" he asked.

"No, sir."

"I thought not. You look more of the southern blood."

Alfred returned the earnest gaze of his companion, and he soon made up his mind that he had nothing to fear, for the old gentleman was kind looking, and his voice was smooth and mild.

"You mustn't think me impertinent," resumed the stranger, "but really I would like to know from what part of England you come?"

"If I were at home, sir, I should be in Devonshire."

"Ah, then you were born in Devonshire?"

The speaker seemed disappointed.

Alfred hesitated. At length a vague idea broke over his mind that the stranger might have discovered some family likeness in his countenance, and a dim ray of hope broke in upon his soul.

"I do not know that I was born in Devonshire, sir; but I was brought up in that county."

The old man sat down his coffee-cup and wiped his mouth, and then he looked again into Alfred's face.

"I'm making myself interested on a short acquaintance," he said, while a faint smile rested upon his features; "but the truth is, your features put me in mind of one whom I once knew. Will you tell me what you know of your birth-place?"

"Nothing, sir," returned Alfred, in an earnest, anxious tone.

"What of your parents, then?"

"Nothing."

"Of your early life, then?"

"At four years of age, sir, I was cast away upon Little Devon Head. I was saved from the wreck by the light-keeper there, and with him I lived till about a year ago."

"There isn't much light in that," uttered the old gentleman. "You don't know whom you were with previous to your being cast away?"

"Yes, sir. It was a man who called himself my father. His name was Marrok Pettrell."

"Now you talk!" exclaimed the stranger, with a sudden energy. "I' faith, I'm not so wild in my reading features as I had feared. Did you ever come across a companion that this Pettrell had, a fellow named Mark Bronkou?"

"Yes, yes!"

"Can you tell me where those two chaps are now?"

For some time Alfred remained silent. He thought over the events of the past, and at length he made up his mind to tell his whole story to the man before him. The recital could in no way endanger himself, and it might benefit him; so he related the principal events of the past year, together with the present whereabouts of the smuggler, and his recent escape from her.

The old gentleman thumped upon the table with the handle of his knife for several moments after Alfred had concluded his story.

"Now tell me, sir," said the youth, with trembling voice, "what you know of me or mine?"

"That scamp of a Pettrell is no more your father than I am."

"But of my father—my true father—can you tell me?"

"Not anything that you would wish at present to know."

"Anything—anything would bless me."

"You are not so sure of that, my young man," said the old gentleman, as he arose from the table. "I will help you, however; and in the end I think you will find I am the most wise."

chaise is waiting, and I must be off. You can easily reach Ravenglass by noon, and there you will find a coach for Lancaster. When there you will take the mail coach on the great Manchester road, and your route will be direct. Don't fail, now, to do as I have bid. I will look up matters for you when I return. Have you money enough to carry you through?"

"Yes, sir."

"Then take care of yourself. You will find your confidence in me worth more than

ALFRED'S BREAKFAST, AND A STRANGE ACQUAINTANCE.

He touched the table bell as he spoke, and the landlord soon made his appearance.

"Let me have pen, ink and paper," said the stranger.

The materials were soon brought, and the old gentleman sat down to the table and wrote. When the note was finished he folded and directed it.

"Here," he said, "take this and make your way to London without delay. Here is my card. Go to my house, hand the note to my secretary, and there you will remain till I return. I am on my way now to Carlisle, and shall be back in two weeks. My

you think for. Good-by, till I see you again."

The old gentleman left the room as he spoke and entered his chaise. The postilion whipped up the horses, and they moved off at a quick pace. Alfred watched the vehicle till it was lost to his sight, and then he bent his eyes to the floor, and remained for a long time in a state of trembling, ambiguous thought. "Who am I, who is my father? What can this stranger know of my parentage?" These questions kept constantly recurring, to the exclusion of every other thought.

CHAPTER IX.

DAYLIGHT VANISHES AGAIN.

ALFRED was at length aroused from his reverie by the voice of his landlord, who wished to know if he had finished his breakfast.

"Zounds!" uttered the publican, as he began to clear away the dishes, "you've had an honor. I offered to set the admiral another table, but he said he'd eat with you. He's as kind-hearted a man as there be between here and Land's End. Engaged you in his service, haint he?"

"Service," repeated Alfred, looking up into the landlord's face.

"Yes. Didn't Sir William speak about your stopping with him?"

"Ah, yes. I understand. Yes—yes," returned Alfred, who now saw what the inquisitive landlord was after.

"Lucky fellow—zounds! Wish I was in his service. Comes up here every summer to visit his estates in Cumberland. Gives me a guinea, always."

As soon as Alfred got clear of the landlord, he examined the card he had received from the old gentleman. In one corner was a seal bearing a coat of arms, and below it was written with a pencil:—

SIR WILLIAM BRENT—ADMIRAL,
13 Hanover Square, London.

The note was addressed to "Donald McIvar, Secretary," and bore the same direction.

Of course Alfred could only wonder what was to be the end of all this, and of course he resolved to make his way as soon as possible to London. He felt perfectly assured that the old baronet had not and would not deceive him. He settled his bill for breakfast, and asked what time the stage-coach would leave Ravenglass for the south.

"Half an hour after noon," returned the landlord. "But you can have a post-chaise from here."

"That wouldn't help me, for I should have to wait at Ravenglass for the coach."

"Certain."

"Then I'll go on foot. I shall have a better chance to see the country."

"Well, you'll reach there afore the coach, easy enough."

Shortly afterwards the youth set forward, and as soon as he had got clear of the inn he quickened his pace. At the distance of two miles he came to a point where the road entered a deep wood, and he could hear the low murmuring of the sea as it broke upon the rocks of the coast to his right. He had been in the wood but a short time when he saw two men seated on a rock by the roadside, at some distance ahead. They were two stout countrymen by their looks, and without fear the youth approached them. There was a quick whispering between them as Alfred came near, and when he had reached the place, they slipped down from the rock and joined him.

"Good morning," said one of the men.

Alfred returned the compliment without stopping, and the two men kept along with him.

"How far are you from this morning?"

"From Egremont," returned the youth, showing by his manner that he was not desirous of company.

"Belong in Egremont?"

"No."

The two men changed significant glances.

"D'ye know anything 'bout the 'Adder'?"

"'Adder'!" repeated Alfred with a start.

"Yes."

"What do you mean?"

"Mean the 'Adder'. Don't you know her?"

Our hero began to tremble. The men were both strangers to him, and yet he feared they had some clew to his real character. He determined to keep his own counsel, however.

"If you will speak more plainly," he returned, "perhaps I can understand you."

He could see that the men exchanged glances again.

"S'pose we was excisemen, or somethin' o' that sort, couldn't you tell us where the 'Adder' was?"

"No. Does that satisfy you?"

"Not quite, 'cause I believe you know all 'bout her."

Alfred felt like knocking the fellow down, but he restrained his passion.

"Look here," said the second man, "do ye not know that the 'Adder' is a smuggler?"

"Look ye, fellows; what do you mean by your impertinent questions? If you have business this way, I beg you will pass on and leave me to myself."

As our hero spoke, the two men fell behind, and he hurried forward. He could hear the fellows earnestly talking, and he noticed that they followed him. A short distance further brought him to an abrupt turn in the road, and some fifteen or twenty rods ahead, he saw two more men just coming out from the wood from the direction of the sea. They stopped as they noticed the youth, and those behind seemed to make some signal to them.

Alfred now began to feel sure that some plan was on foot for his recapture. He had no weapon, and his heart sank within him as he thought of being carried back to the brig. The wood offered him no means of escape, and with a trembling step he kept on. The two men who were ahead came out into the road as he approached, and one of them stepped directly in front of him.

"What do you want?" asked Alfred.

"Want to ask ye a question. Aint you Alfred Pettrell?"

"No!"

"Harrold, ye know the captain said he'd call hisself," interposed the other. "Aint yer name Harrold?"

Alfred gathered all his strength for one trial. With one blow of his fist he knocked the man down in front of him, and then set off at the top of his speed.

"Stop! stop!" yelled the men, as they started in pursuit.

Alfred turned his head and saw that the other two had come up, and that the man he had levelled was getting upon his feet.

"Stop, or we'll fire into you!" shouted one of the pursuers.

The youth did not stop, but rather increased his speed.

"Stop, or we'll fire!"

No notice was taken of the threat, and in a moment more a pistol ball came whizzing by Alfred's head.

Another ball came—and another, but the youth was unharmed. He was satisfied that he could easily outrun his pursuers, and he kept on. Just after the third ball whizzed by him he turned his head, and saw that the fourth man had stopped and was levelling his heavy pistol. He heard the report, and on the same instant he felt a twinge in the calf of his leg. He ran a few steps further, but his leg failed him, and he could only limp along, and ere long a heavy hand was laid upon his shoulder.

"I guess you won't run much further, my young covey," exclaimed the fellow who had stopped him.

"Tell me what you want of me," said Alfred, as he found the four men gathered about him.

"We want you to go back where ye run away from last night. Capt'n Pettrell don't think you served him a werry pooty trick."

"And you are deputized to carry me back to the brig," said Alfred, in a desponding tone.

"Sartin. That's what we've come for; so you'll just go along with us to the shore."

Alfred saw that his captors were not the kind of men with whom any argument or persuasion would be profitable, and he also saw that his hope of escape was entirely cut off, so he turned slowly about, and was led back. He learned that his escape had been discovered at two o'clock, when the watch was relieved, and that word had been immediately sent on shore to the captain, who at once sent the four men in a sail-boat to make their way down the coast to a point south of the mouth of the Eden; and from thence they had directions to go on shore and lie in wait on the road. A fresh and favorable breeze had brought the boat down in good season, and the men had been on the watch over an hour when the youth came along. Other men had been sent in different directions, but the bird had been caught in the very direction Pettrell had anticipated.

Alfred's leg pained him considerably, and it was with difficulty that he made his way along. At first he refused the assistance that was tendered him; but ere long he was glad to accept of it, and with a stout arm on either side to support him, he found his labor lighter. When the party arrived at the rock where Alfred met the first two men, they turned into the wood and moved toward the sea-shore.

"You mustn't blame us," said one of the men, as soon as they had turned out from the highway. "As sure as heaven we are sorry you be hurt, but we couldn't help it. 'Twould not do for you to run away and blow, yer see."

"I had no intention of betraying"——

Alfred hesitated, for he remembered what he had told Sir William.

"Pettrell was afeared you would," said the man who had spoken before. "But you know we couldn't help what we did. You wouldn't stop."

The youth doubted whether the speaker was moved by sympathy, or whether he was only afraid Pettrell would blame him for the wound that had been given to the prisoner. At any rate, the men did not seem to be really evil-disposed, only they were rough and uncouth by nature and education, and their connection with the smugglers rendered them fearful of detection, which Pettrell had given them to understand would follow from Alfred's being at liberty.

At length the sea-coast was reached, and Alfred was assisted into the boat which lay there. His leg now began to swell, and the pain was intense. The ball seemed to be lodged among the cords, for the least movement rendered the torture excruciating, but he bore it the best way he could. Occasionally, as the boat was on her course, he dipped his hand overboard and bathed the parts about the wound, and that afforded him slight relief.

It was an hour after noon when the boat reached the brig, and instead of finding himself on the Lancashire stage, our hero was once more doomed to his prison house on board the smuggler.

"Wounded, eh?" uttered Pettrell, as the poor youth was helped over the gangway.

"We couldn't help it, sir," said one of the captors. "He run, and we couldn't do anything but wing him."

"Good enough for him," said Pettrell.

For an instant Alfred forgot his pain in the fire of indignation that burned in his bosom, as he met the cold, demoniac look of the smuggler captain.

"It won't be safe for you to try that game again, my boy," continued Pettrell. "The pitcher that goes to the well once too often gets broken! Once more will be once too often for you to try this game."

Alfred made no reply, but groaned in pain.

"I guess the ball's in his leg now," said the fellow who had fired the pistol that did the damage.

"Here, Waffon, you are surgeon enough for this job," said Pettrell. "Take the youngster below, and fix him up the best way you can. If the ball is there, get it out. You've done worse jobs than that."

Waffon acknowledged the compliment, and then followed Alfred down into the cabin.

The smuggler was not so bad a surgeon as might have been supposed from the coarse remark of Pettrell, for he was careful in his handling of the wound, and he displayed much skill in the use of the simple instruments he had at hand. The ball was found lodged among the large tendons just below the back part of the knee joint, and Waffon extracted it with but little cutting. Then the wound was bandaged, and Alfred was helped into his berth.

It was three weeks before our hero could walk comfortably, and at the end of that time the brig was got under way for sea. Alfred heard that there had been a disturbance of some kind on shore, in which the smugglers bore a part, and he heard the name of Sir William used; but most of the excisemen in the vicinity were hired to the smugglers' interest, and the affair had passed off without much trouble.

The brig had taken in a large stock of provisions, and her complement of men was again made up to its former number. Alfred had learned that the smuggler's destination was again for the East Indies, and he saw another inevitable year of galling bondage before him.

CHAPTER X.

PIRATES.

WHEN the smugglers reached the Indies they commenced a new system of operations. A lucrative opportunity was offered to them for the smuggling of opium into Canton. Their opium was mostly procured in Calcutta, and for two years they followed this business.

Those were two long years for Alfred Harrold. Not once during that time had he set his foot on shore, nor was there a single opportunity for his escape. He had become sick and weary, and more than once he had almost determined to join fully with his companions; but the memory of his youthful hopes still clung about his soul, and he had conquered the feeling. He had breasted the storm, and his face was still turned towards the beacon of his young aspirations. Pettrell was the same as ever—stern and unfeeling—and seeming to exult in the misery he saw Alfred suffering.

Mark Bronkon scarcely ever spoke to the young man, except when business required it. He had grown more morose in his manner, and his features were still darker in their shadowing of passion.

Alfred had seen his nineteenth birthday, and he was fast verging towards the sum of life that was to make up his twenty years on earth. He had grown more of the man in form and feature, and there were few on board the brig who could equal him in physical strength. He had almost forgotten the circumstance of having met Sir William Brent, and when he thought of it, it was as an event of the past which might never have effect in the future.

One day, while the brig lay at the outer extremity of Canton Bay, three dark-looking men came on board and went with Pettrell and Bronkon into the cabin, where they remained in close consultation for half an hour. At the end of that time, Waffon was called down, and soon afterwards ten more of the men were sent for. When the meeting was broken up the three strangers departed, and there were strange and mysterious whisperings about the deck. Alfred mistrusted that some new scheme of mischief was on foot, but he could get no clue to its character.

At night the brig's anchors were hove up and sail was made, and the next morning she was anchored in a small bay of one of the Larron Islands, some eighty miles south of Canton. Not far from where the smuggler had anchored lay an old dismasted brig, and ere long a boat put off from her side containing the three men who had visited the "Adder" the previous day.

Another consultation was held, and when the strangers left the brig, Bronkon and Waffon went with them. In two hours more Alfred saw that heavy guns were being hoisted out from the wreck, and ere long they were brought alongside of the smuggler. The youth experienced a stunning sensation as the thought first broke upon him that Pettrell was about to turn pirate.

Before night, ten guns had been brought on board the brig, and rigged upon their carriages. They were eighteen pounders, and port-holes were knocked open to receive them. Large boxes of ammunition were brought from the wreck, together with two large chests of small arms; and, to cap the climax, fourteen strange men were added to the brig's crew!

It was late at night when the brig was again got under way, and as soon as she was fairly clear of the island, Pettrell called Alfred into the cabin. Bronkon was there, but no one else besides those three.

"Alfred," said the captain, "can you imagine the nature of the business we are going at?"

The young man had no fear of Pettrell now; he had raised himself above the fear of one so base, and he replied calmly:—

"I have suspected your plans, sir; but I may be wrong."

"Perhaps not. Let us hear what you have suspected."

"I have suspected that you were about to commit the crime piracy."

Alfred could not repress the cold shudder that crept over him as he pronounced that terrible word, and a wicked smile broke over the features of Marrok Pettrell.

"You have hit the nail exactly on the head," returned the latter; "and since that part of the business is disposed of, I'll whisper a few words of counsel in your ear."

The captain glanced at Bronkon, and then while a look of deadly meaning settled upon his hard features, he continued:—

"I know, my young man, that you are hardly reconciled yet to the company you keep, and I often see that soft morality of yours making its way into notice. You have been a good sailor, and I have let you have pretty much your own way so far; but you have got to turn over a new leaf now. I want no more of your morality, nor will I hear any more of your whims about sin. It is all stuff! We are now under a free flag, and you have got to be one of us. We've got some new men, too, who are used to the business, and who mustn't see the white feather in you. Now, Master Alfred, the whole business can be summed up in a few words. You've got to be one of us—fare as the rest do—bear your part of the duty that may turn up, and never drop a word in the hearing of the men that you do not like our doings."

"Have you finished?" calmly asked the young man.

"Yes."

"Then I may speak?"

"Certainly; but you had better exercise care."

"I shall speak as freely as you have done," said Alfred, not at all daunted by the threatening look of the captain.

"Very well. Go on."

"Then, sir, so long as I am forced to remain on board this brig, I shall do my duty as a seaman, but I will never raise my hand as a pirate."

"Better be careful!" growled Bronkon.

"I shall be very careful that the sin of piracy rests not on my soul."

For a few moments Pettrell and Bronkon regarded each other in silence.

"Look ye," said the captain, while his frame trembled with passion; "we have laws on board this vessel, and for him that breaks them the yard-arm shall find a hanging place!"

"Very well," calmly replied Alfred.

"Better be careful!" again growled Bronkon.

"I don't believe you'll run the risk of getting your neck stretched," added Pettrell. "But let me assure you that it wouldn't go against my grain at all to do the job for you, if you attempt to breed mutiny."

"I have no reason to doubt your word," said Alfred.

"Of course you haven't."

"Nor do I."

"Then you will be wise if you govern yourself accordingly."

"It is not always wise to be governed by every wind that blows. You wouldn't think of keeping square yards and running off before the ever-changing gale."

"None of your morality."

"I do not give it for your benefit, but only to show you my rule of conduct. Now you can do with your brig as you choose, and I shall do as I choose. I am not here of my own free will, but am forced to my present position. There is a bound, however, beyond which I cannot be forced. I trust you understand me?"

"I do understand you; but I don't believe you understand me!"

As Pettrell thus spoke, he arose from his seat and laid his hand upon the young man's head. His features were tortured into a fearful expression, and his words were hissed out like the voice of a serpent.

"Mark me," he said; "if you dare to show a look of insubordination before the men, you'll hang for it!"

Marrok Pettrell turned and went on deck.

"Youngster, you'd better be careful!" uttered Bronkon.

"Stop, Mark Bronkon," exclaimed the youth, as the dark-looking mate started to leave the cabin. "I once saved your life, and to do it, I took the lives of two men who were doing but their duty. At that moment, when you were bent helpless over the trunk, and the sword was at your breast, I pitied you in your utter helplessness, and saved you. Now will you lend your hand to crush me? I seek the harm of no man. Were I at this moment clear of the brig, no word of mine should betray her character; but I cannot become a pirate. Why should I be forced to this thing? Can you tell me why I am thus trampled upon? why thus abused? What harm have I done? what evil thought or deed have I given?"

"I don't know," gruffly returned Bronkon.

"Have I given any?"

"I couldn't tell you."

"Ah, Bronkon, you may sneer at my young hopes—at my soul's expression of its desired rectitude—but if you ever entertained a single youthful aspiration that has been crushed, you should know how to pity me. Perhaps you never did—perhaps your life was always cast in the rough paths you now tread."

"Stuff! Gammon!" growled Bronkon; and yet Alfred thought he saw a tear rolling down the dark man's cheek. But he turned away to hide it.

"Can you not tell me"——

Bronkon stopped not to hear the youth speak further, but with an uneasy movement he turned away and went on deck.

"Can it be possible," uttered Alfred to himself, "that Bronkon has one tender feeling in his bosom? That was certainly a tear I saw upon his cheek—and he surely trembled while I spoke."

The young man arose from his seat and began to pace the cabin. The full realization of his situation had come upon him, and he trembled as he thought of the terrible ordeal through which he had got to pass. But he swerved not from his resolution to keep his hands clear of the fatal work that had been planned. He had not long for his reflections, however, for as soon as the brig's course had been laid out, and the watch set, the captain and one of the strangers came down.

"You'd better turn in," said Pettrell, as he cast a wicked glance upon Alfred; "for you'll have to go on deck at midnight. You are still in my watch."

Alfred got into his berth, but it was a long time before he fell asleep, and when the drowsy fit did come upon him, he left Pettrell and the new man engaged in consulting the chart of the Indian Ocean. This newcomer was a villanous fellow, and his name was Dunham—at least, so Pettrell called him, and he had been an officer of a pirate vessel that had been cast away on the island where the "Adder" had taken him in.

At midnight, Alfred went on deck, and he found that the brig was heading for the Straits of Sunda, and that she was to make the best of her way into the Indian Ocean. Half-a-dozen of the men were at work in the forward bunk-room making cartridges, and some of the hands on deck were set to work lashing up stands of grape-shot.

At two o'clock, Alfred took the helm, and shortly afterwards Pettrell came on deck to look at the compass.

"Got over your spleen?" said the captain.

"Don't try to worry me, sir, when there is no occasion for it," retorted Alfred.

"Then don't give me occasion."

Just then Dunham came aft, and Pettrell turned away from the binnacle. The youth overheard most of their conversation, and from it he learned that no operations of a decided character were to be commenced till the brig had cleared the China Sea; but that after the Straits of Sunda were passed, it was their intention to throw themselves upon the first merchantman they might fall in with. But that would be two weeks, at least, in the future, and our hero was informed by Pettrell, as the latter turned again towards him, that he "would have plenty of time for reflection."

CHAPTER XI.

THE SHIP.—THE TRUE HERO.

In three weeks from the time of the taking in of the brig's piratical armament, she had entered the Indian Ocean, and was standing down towards the Cape of Good Hope. The duty had thus far been of a quiet and steady character, and though the reckless crew saw nothing out of the way in the demeanor of Alfred Harrold, yet he had become firmly fixed in his determination to die ere he would lay his hand to the consummation of any robbery upon the high seas.

One thing seemed to give Marrok Pettrell more occasion for troublous feelings than all else, and that was, the general disposition of the crew towards loving his unwilling protege. The rough seamen could not but love the young man, for he was always mild and kind, and he never failed to offer his assistance where it could benefit a shipmate. Some of them he had taught to read, and to some he had imparted instruction in navigation. Those uneducated children of sin and shame had learned to look upon the youth with respect and esteem, for he never lost sight of his true dignity, and yet he always associated with his shipmates upon terms of social equality. The coarse and profane jest he passed unheeded by, while he smiled at the wit of his companions.

Few men are so sunken that they will not love that which is to them kind and generous, and which at the same time meets them upon a social equality. There are some, to be sure, in whose bosoms the spark of gratitude cannot exist; but generally it is because the cold hand of some bitter disappointment or dire revenge lies heavily there. At any rate, there were few on board the brig who did not love the pale youth who read to them, and who taught them. They had no appreciation of his peculiar moral qualities, but his social nature was congenial. Pettrell saw it all, and often did his teeth grate like files as he found that Alfred was making so many friends among the crew.

Early one morning, after the brig had passed the southern tropic, the crew were aroused by the reporting of a sail. Pettrell sprang up from the cabin with his glass, and he quickly had the sail in view. It proved to be a ship standing to the southward and westward.

"A homeward-bound Indiaman," said Dunham.

"She will be a rich prize," said Bronkon.

"And perhaps a hard one to take," suggested the captain.

"Never fear for that," resumed Dunham. "We are forty—yes, forty-one, all told—and I doubt if the ship has much over half that number. She may have passengers, but they won't be likely to do much."

Pettrell was all excitement. He hurried about the deck to see that all was in order for the chase, and then he came aft and used his glass again.

The ship had been seen when daylight first fairly broke, and she was not now more than four miles distant. The wind was nearly east. The ship was dead to leeward of the brig, and standing across the line of the latter's course.

"Let's have the stun'-sails on, Bronkon," said the captain. "By heavens, that fellow sails low!"

The studding-sails were set both sides, and the starboard clue of the mainsail set. The brig was now dead before the wind, but ere long she was put three points to the southward, and her starboard studding-sails taken in. It was soon evident that she was gaining on the ship.

"There goes her stun'-sails," uttered Bronkon. "She smells danger."

"I don't wonder," said Dunham. "I rather guess they know what we mean."

"Waffon," said Pettrell, "get up grog enough for all hands. Let 'em have a strong pull."

"That's the talk," added Dunham, with a satisfied chuckle. "Noth'n like rum to make men fight. It makes 'em savage like."

After the expression of this weighty opinion, Dunham took the glass and examined the ship, and ere long the grog-tub was brought upon deck.

"Help yourselves, my men," said Pettrell, "only be careful and don't get enough to lay you by the scuppers."

Alfred now felt that his hour of trial had come, but he nerved himself for the contest, and he felt strong in his resolution.

"Won't you have a dip at the tub?" asked Pettrell.

"No," returned our hero.

"You had better," urged the pirate captain, while a demon sparkled in his eye.

"I don't wish for it, sir."

"It will do you good."

"I do not wish for it."

"It will make you fight better."

"All my fighting can be done without it."

"Then you won't fight, eh?"

"I cannot tell yet."

"But if there is need of it?"

"Let the need come, and I shall not be behind."

"But look ye, Master Alfred, beware that you don't set yourself up as judge of that need. I'll tell you when the need comes."

"Better fight," said Bronkon.

"Of course he will," added Pettrell, "I don't believe he wants to swing quite yet."

"Alfred, you can fight and you must," said Bronkon, in a low tone, after the captain had turned away.

"You know my resolutions," calmly returned our hero.

"Oh, bah! Stuff! Gammon! It's all nonsense to throw your life away. Do not, for God's sake, be a fool!"

Alfred was startled by the strange manner of Bronkon. He gazed into the mate's dark features, but he could only see the same hard, cold expression that generally rested there.

"Don't be a fool!" repeated Bronkon, as he turned away.

Two hours had passed since the chase began, and the brig was within a quarter of a mile of the ship. Upon the quarter-deck of the latter quite a body of people were collected, and many of them were passengers— some females.

"I don't think there'll be much resistance," said Dunham, as he stopped and watched the movements of Bronkon, who was looking through the glass.

"I don't know," returned the latter, still gazing through the instrument. "I can see the glitter of arms, and the captain is certainly mustering his passengers. Yes, there are cutlasses and pistols. By the jumping cokey, we shall have work yet!"

"Never mind, if we get enough to pay us," said Dunham. "Can't expect always to win without losing a cast. Them passengers won't be much."

"Fire a gun, Waffon," ordered Pettrell. "We'll see if she will lay to."

The gun was fired, but the ship still stood on.

"Give 'em a shot, Waffon, and see if that will fetch 'em," cried the captain, who was growing more excited, as he saw the rich prize so near to his grasp. "In with a double-header, Waffon, and give it to her among her rigging."

The shot was fired, but without effect.

"You want practice," said Dunham; "let me try a hand."

A bow gun was levelled, Dunham took sight and fired, and on the next instant a cloud of splinters was seen flying about the ship's quarter-deck.

"If that doesn't stop 'em," uttered Pettrell, "I will luff and give them a broadside."

There was no need of the pirate's threat being carried into execution, however, for the ship braced her fore and mizzen yards up, and came into the wind with her main-topsail aback.

"They're ready to show fight," exclaimed Bronkon. "Her crew are armed with pikes, and the passengers have cutlasses. The women have gone below."

"We're a match for them," returned Pettrell. "Stand by, my men. We'll luff and run afoul of her weather quarter. Let every man have his cutlass in his right hand and a pistol in his left, and spring for her bulwarks the moment we touch. Catch your cutlasses in your teeth if you want a hand to help you over her side. Here, Alfred, if you are afraid of powder, take the wheel;

you can do well there." The youth did not move.

"Take the wheel, I say!" cried Pettrell.

"Not to help you in reaching that ship," firmly returned Alfred.

"What! Do you refuse? Take the wheel, I say!"

"Never!"

"By your life, youngster, if you don't take that wheel, you'll rue it."

"I shall not take it, sir, nor shall I move a finger towards furthering your designs upon that ship."

"Alfred," hissed the pirate captain, with fearful emphasis, "if—you—don't—take—that—wheel—you—shall—swing!"

Alfred trembled, and a pallor stole over his countenance, but he moved not.

"Take it!" said Bronkon.

"No," resolutely returned the youth; and as he spoke he folded his arms across his breast.

Pettrell foamed with rage, and with a demoniac growl he sprang upon the young man and bore him to the deck.

"Come, come, Marrok," cried Bronkon, "we've got other fish to fry now. Let the man keep the wheel that's got it. Here we are. Death and destruction! Spring to the braces! in the lee braces, quick! Down with it! Come, come, Marrok, be captain if you are going to!"

Marrok Pettrell sprang to his feet, and he saw how much need there was of his attention to the affairs of his vessel, for she was already within half a dozen fathoms of the ship. He was still mad with rage, and it was some time before he could command himself; but the necessity for action soon called him to his senses.

The brig had luffed so as to fall afoul of the ship, and when she touched, the men poured up the Indiaman's side, with Bronkon and Pettrell at their head. They received the fire of the merchantman's crew with but little damage, and having knocked the pikes aside, they leaped upon the deck.

The struggle was of short duration, and in less than ten minutes from the time of the pirates' boarding, they were masters of the ship. No violence was offered after the crew had surrendered, save a few revengeful passes among the heated seamen. Four of the ship's men were killed, and quite a number wounded. The pirate lost five men, three having been shot in boarding.

Alfred Harrold remained the sole occupant of the brig, and more than once the thought occurred to him of cutting the grapplings and letting the ship drop off, and of then letting the brig run with himself alone on board; but the plan was impracticable, and he dropped it. He saw the conflict, and he saw a tiny stream of blood starting from one of the Indiaman's scuppers; and he thanked God that he was not there. But then came the thought of the pirate chieftain's threat, and with a shudder his eye rested upon the fore-yard arm.

"Let it come," he murmured to himself. "God will not forsake me, even though they kill this poor body. They cannot harm the soul."

Alfred heard the ship's crew cry for quarter, and in a few moments more Bronkon and half a dozen men returned to the brig's deck and removed the hatches. Shortly afterwards a whip was rove upon the merchantman's main-yard-arm, and another upon the mainstay, and then the pirates began to hoist out such articles of value as they took a fancy for. Three boxes of money were found beneath the floor of the ship's cabin, and much jewelry was taken from the passengers.

In two hours after the ship had surrendered, the pirates returned to their own vessel, and she was allowed to proceed on her way.

"That's better than buying a cargo," said Pettrell, as the hatches were closed over the valuables.

"Fact," said Bronkon.

"You have bought these things of one who will take a terrible pay!" uttered Alfred Harrold.

None heard him save Bronkon. The dark man gazed into the youth's face, and a change came over his features.

"That's all stuff!" he said, with an effort

to look the contempt he spoke, but which was unsuccessful.

"'Tis fearfully bought!" said Alfred. The mate heard him, and then turned away. Ere long the brig was clear, and with flowing sheets she went dashing off towards the Cape of Good Hope.

CHAPTER XII.
THE YARD-ARM.

THE afternoon had passed half away when everything was arranged for the examination and stowing away of the plunder. Pettrell was walking the quarter-deck with quick, nervous strides, and his fists were clutched together till the finger nails almost penetrated the flesh. The men regarded him in silence, and an ominous stillness reigned throughout the brig.

Bronkon was standing by the binnacle, and upon his face the darkness had grown more deep than ever. He raised his eyes ever and anon from the compass, and cast a glance upon the captain; and once he looked upon Alfred. His features looked more terrible than did those of Pettrell.

Alfred Harrold stood by the starboard quarter rail, and though he felt assured that he was soon to be brought to an account with Pettrell, yet he was calm and collected, and no one could know from his outward appearance, that he had anything to fear.

"Waffon," said the captain, stopping in his walk, and speaking through his clenched teeth, "see that the starboard fore-clew-garnet and buntlines are manned. I want the lee clew of the sail hauled up, sir."

Again Pettrell paced the deck, and without a word of answer or comment his order was obeyed.

"Dunham," he said, as soon as the lee clew of the foresail was up, "send some of the foretopmen aloft, and have a tail-block made fast to the lee fore-yard-arm. Then have a whip rove, sir, with both ends inboard."

This order was obeyed in silence, and the men anxiously awaited the further movements of their chieftain.

"Make a slip-noose in the outer end of that whip, sir, and rig a snatch-block for the running end, and reeve it."

All hands knew well enough the nature of the captain's intentions, and various were the expressions upon the faces of the crew.

"Now, sir," uttered Pettrell, as he turned towards Alfred, "your hour has come. I told you you should swing if you refused to do your duty. You had fair warning—you've had warnings enough—and yet you choose to disobey. Now, sir, I will keep my word. If you have prayers to say, say them!"

The young man's features grew paler as the pirate captain thus addressed him, and there was a tremor upon his lips. The presence of the death sentence, and the sight of the apparatus for carrying it into execution, had more effect than our hero had thought. There was something terrible in such a death; and then, too, to die among such people, with no sympathy, no love, no regret; to fall where a mourner's tear could never drop to his memory, and where no requiem could sound over his grave save the howl of the storm-wind and the tempest. The poor youth had not the fortitude he had counted upon. He could have laid down calmly upon the bed of death had God called him home, but all about him now was so horrible he shrank away in fear.

"Come," said Pettrell, "I am waiting for you. This is a death of your own choosing. You have been warned of it times enough."

"Warned of it!" exclaimed Alfred, clasping his hands in agony. "How have I been warned of it?"

"How? In every way. But a few hours ago I told you you should swing if you did not take that wheel. In the presence of my whole crew you boldly trampled upon my authority. How have I warned you? You know very well how I have warned you. Come, say your prayers, for I suppose one so religious as you must have prayers to say!"

"Marrok Pettrell, I do not believe you

mean to hang me. I cannot believe you will be so heartlessly cruel."

A bitter sneer broke over the pirate's face, and he pointed to where the whip was rove at the yard-arm.

"That—rope—is—for—you!" he uttered, in distinctly separate and emphasized parts. "All the powers of heaven and earth should not make it otherwise. Now rig yourself for it. All here know it's your own choice."

"O Pettrell, do not add base falsehood to your brutal cruelty!" exclaimed Alfred. "Do not tell these men a lie. You dragged me on board this brig—you robbed me of home, of friends, of happiness, and of peace; and you have tried to rob me of honor. You have trampled upon me in your strength, because I was weak. I would not give you my soul's purest jewel—its sacred virtue—and hence you would murder me. I call on all here to witness that I have ever done my duty, as an honest seaman, well and faithfully. These men know that I have ever been"——

"Silence!" thundered Pettrell, for he saw that the youth's words were making an impression upon the crew.

"No, no, Marrok Pettrell. If I am to die you shall not manacle my tongue. What I have said is true. You have stripped my life of all that made it valuable on earth, and because you could not tear from it all that would be valuable in heaven, you would kill me. I speak the truth in this, and I call on God to bear me witness that you have longed, ay, prayed for a pretext for my murder! Now you have it."

"Now you've said enough."

"Perhaps I have."

"And according to your belief," ironically added Pettrell, "you are much fitter for heaven than for earth."

In an instant the expression upon Alfred Harrold's face was changed. The fear-marks passed away, and all was calm again.

"I can commend myself to the care of God without fear," he uttered.

"Then come!"

Pettrell moved forward as he spoke, and Alfred followed him.

"Now, sir, your time is up," the pirate captain said.

"Very well. But before I die let me"——

"Silence! Not another word. Your tongue has wagged enough. Here!"

As Pettrell spoke, he took the noose from the breech of one of the guns, and threw it over Alfred's head.

At that moment Mark Bronkon started up from the spot where he had been leaning by the binnacle, and came forward. He trembled from head to foot, and a strange expression was upon his countenance.

"Marrok," he said, "let this thing be stopped! Take that rope from his neck!"

"S'death! What do you mean, Mark?" uttered Pettrell, in astonishment.

"I mean that the young man shall not die!"

"Are you crazy?"

"No, I'm in sober earnest."

"Then stand back; for, by my salvation, the fellow shall die! Man the whip! Man the whip, I say!"

Not a soul moved to obey the order.

"Man the whip, and run the mutineer up!" shouted the pirate captain, foaming with rage.

"No, no, Marrok Pettrell," said Bronkon, in a deep calm tone. "Not a man shall touch that rope. The youngster saved my life once, and now I'll save his. What he has said is true."

"By heavens, Mark, you had better beware!" uttered Pettrell, turning towards his mate.

"Don't speak too much," he said in a whisper. "You know me, Marrok, too well for that."

"Man the whip."

Not a man moved, and on the next instant Pettrell drew a pistol, but Bronkon knocked it from his hand.

The attention of the crew was now turned from the doomed youth to the dark-faced mate. The men trembled as they saw the rage of their chieftain, but a sort of awe stole over them when they saw the stout form of Bronkon towering in its strength.

One of them slipped the rope from Alfred's neck, but Pettrell saw it not.

"Marrok," said the mate, as he knocked the pistol down, "let this thing stop where it is. I have said that Alfred shall not die. You know me well enough to think no more of the deed."

"Mark, that boy is mine!"

"——sh! Say no more."

"But he is mine."

"Not to kill."

"Blood and destruction! Mark, what do you mean? Stand back and let this thing go on. Ha! who took off the rope? Put it on again. Put it on, I say. The first man that disobeys me shall die!"

"O fool!" muttered Bronkon, as he laid his hand on Pettrell's shoulder. "Come aft a moment for I would speak a word in your ear."

The mate half dragged the captain to the quarter-deck, and there they remained in earnest conversation several minutes. At length Bronkon came forward.

"Hark ye, my men," he said. "The captain will abide by your decision. Shall the young man die?"

Nearly all the crew spoke as one man, and a thundering "No!" broke upon the air.

Mark Bronkon laid his hand upon Alfred's shoulder, and led him towards the quarter-deck.

"Alfred," said he, "you have been a fool; but I owed you one, and I have paid it. We are square now. For the future you must look out for yourself."

"Oh, God will bless you for this!" ejaculated the youth.

"Will he?"

"Yes, yes. And I will bless you as long as I live."

Bronkon turned away without further remark, and shortly afterwards Alfred sought the cabin. He sank upon his knees as soon as he found himself alone, and offered up to God his soul's prayer. A foot-step on the ladder aroused him. It was Marrok Pettrell.

"Alfred," said the captain, as he sank into a seat almost exhausted by the effects of the rage he had held in his bosom, "this has been done to please Mark Bronkon. You saved him once, and he has now saved you; but, as sure as there is a God in Heaven, there shall be no second respite. Cross me but once again, and your death is as sure as though you hung by the neck from the yard-arm!"

Alfred made no reply. He buried his face in his hands, and for a long time he was lost to everything save the scene just passed.

CHAPTER XIII.

THE FATAL SHOT.

THE brig fell in with no more merchant-men until after she had doubled the cape, and it was the intention of Pettrell to proceed directly to England. Alfred's heart leaped with new hope as he heard this, and he resolved that if he could once more get clear of the vessel, he would not be brought back alive. He prayed that the pirates might not attempt to take another prize, but he knew they would if the opportunity were to be afforded. His treatment by the captain had been cold and formal, and as harsh as circumstances would allow. Bronkon scarcely seemed to notice him, and when duty required that the mate should address him, it was always done in a low, growling tone. To our hero the character of Mark Bronkon presented a problem which he could not solve.

Time passed on. Summer had gone, and autumn had commenced. The pirate brig had passed the Cape de Verds without any event to stir the men from the dull monotony of sea-life, and they began to speak of hunting up a prize. Some proposed steering to the westward and lying in wait for some American Indiaman; but Pettrell decided to stand on for old England.

One bright day, while the Peak of Teneriffe was in sight on the starboard bow, a sail was reported on the opposite bow. In a moment all was excitement upon the pirate's deck, and Pettrell seized his glass. It wanted an hour of noon, and the wind was fresh from the westward.

In half an hour the strange sail was made out to be a ship, and in another half-hour she was "hull up," going before the wind, and evidently bound into some of the Canary ports. It was evident that she could be cut off before she could cross the brig's forefoot, and to this end the helm of the latter was put up a spoke.

The pirate's guns were shotted, her arm-chests opened, and as soon as the small arms were all distributed, a gun was fired for the ship to heave to. The ship kept on, and ran up an American flag at her peak.

"We'll give 'em our flag," said Pettrell; and in a few moments more a sable flag fluttered out from the brig's peak. The flag was as black as night, with no relief or device of any kind.

As soon as the flag was shown, another gun was fired, and ere long the ship came into the wind on the starboard tack, and hove to. The pirate was now within a cable's length of the American, and she had made her arrangements to round to under the ship's lee quarter. The men were stationed by the rigging ready for a leap, save such as were needed at the braces, and at length the pirate's yards were braced up, her helm put hard down, and she came boldly around under the high quarter-rail of her intended victim.

Alfred had taken a cutlass and pistols, but he had determined not to use them save in defense of his own life.

"Ha! What is this?" cried Pettrell.

All eyes were turned to the side of the ship just in time to see two heavy guns showing their wide-mouthed muzzles through port-holes that had not been before noticed, the ports having been removed but an instant before the guns were run out.

The pirates discovered their error too late, for while they were huddled together for a leap, the ship's guns belched forth a load of iron hail that made terrific work among them. Wild and loud were the cries and curses that rang out upon the air, and before the pirates had recovered from their shock their brig had fallen off more than two cables' lengths.

Pettrell ran his eyes over the deck, and found that eight of his men were dead.

"Spring to the larboard braces!" he shouted. "Haul them in smartly. Port the helm. We'll board that fellow, if we do it at the cost of half our blood! Work quick!"

The men worked quickly enough, but the brig did not work. She was all aback when she began to drift off, and as her yards came up on the starboard tack with her helm a-port, she just came into the wind and there she stuck. Pettrell stamped and swore, and by the time he got his sails full again, the ship had filled away, and as she came off to her course she brought the brig directly under her larboard beam.

"Good heavens! there come her guns again!" exclaimed Waffon.

And Waffon spoke truly, for on the next instant a twenty-four pound ball came crashing through the brig's mainmast, while a load of grape was rained upon her deck.

Mark Bronkon uttered a low groan of pain, and pressing his hand upon his side he sank back upon the trunk of the cabin companion-way. Alfred sprang to his side and raised him up.

At that instant the mainmast went over the side with a thundering crash, snapping the shrouds off just above the dead-eyes, while the ship stood freely off out of harm's way.

"Are you hurt?" asked Alfred, as he bore the mate up.

"Ah—is that you? Yes, yes. Something struck me here. I feel faint. Help me below."

The mate pressed his hand hard upon his left side as he spoke, and the youth could see the blood trickling out from beneath the large fingers. With a heavy step Bronkon sought the companion-way, and leaning nearly the whole of his weight upon Alfred, he gained his berth.

"There," he murmured, "leave me now, and go on deck. You may be wanted. Send Waffon down as soon as he can be spared. Don't stop—I am well enough now. But—you—may send Waffon down now."

Alfred could see that Bronkon was enduring severe pain, and having handed the suffering man a can of water, he hastened on deck after Waffon.

"Ah! what's in the wind now?" cried Pettrell, as he met Alfred upon the quarter-deck.

"I have carried Bronkon below, sir. He is very badly wounded, I fear."

"The Lord save us! I thought you had been caulking. Poor Bronkon! Well, well, I hope it won't prove fatal. Curse the ship! Go and hunt up Waffon, and send him down."

Waffon was found at work clearing away the wreck made by the fall of the mainmast, and as soon as he heard of Bronkon's accident, he hastened away to attend to his wants, requesting Alfred to accompany and assist him.

The wounded mate was laid upon the cabin table, and removing his clothing, it was found that some kind of shot had entered the second and third false ribs, having broken the third rib. The flesh was considerably lacerated, and a large quantity of blood had escaped. Waffon probed the wound, and soon his wire touched the shot.

"What is it, Waffon?" asked Bronkon, "Will it finish me?"

"I can't tell yet. Can you stand it to have the shot taken out?"

"Yes—anything."

Waffon produced a pair of long-billed forceps, and after much exertion he drew forth the missile, but it caused the patient to utter a sharp cry of pain. It proved to be half of a copper deck-bolt.

"Good gracious!" uttered Bronkon, as he saw the missile; "what a savage thing for a Christian to fire!"

"'Tis an awkward thing," added Waffon, as he placed a clean napkin to the wound to stop the increased flow of blood.

"Tell me the truth," urged the suffering man, "will this finish me?"

"Upon my soul, I cannot tell!" returned Waffon.

"But what do you think?"

"The chances are against you."

"I thought so."

Bronkon's eye rested upon Alfred as he spoke, and a sudden spark lit up its dark depths. He seemed to start with some sudden emotion, and still he gazed into the youth's face. The spark that burned in his eye gradually spread its light over his whole face, and a breaking smile played for an instant about his mouth. It was a calm, quiet smile; very different from that which was to break so bitterly about those curling lips.

"You handle me as though I was a sick baby," he said, at length, his eyes still fixed on the young man.

"I handle you carefully, for I know you must be in pain," returned Alfred.

"It has been many, many years since I have felt a tender hand before. One so rough as I doesn't need it."

"You'll need all the care you can get now," said Waffon, as he pinned together the last bandage, and helped Bronkon into his berth.

"You shall not suffer for the want of it while I am able to care for you," added Alfred.

"I shall live a few days?" he murmured.

"Oh, yes!" assented Waffon.

"Then I am satisfied. Yet 'tis hard to die so; to be hurried off to another world with such a soul as mine! My God! why was I cast upon such a fate?"

There was something in the tone of the suffering man that touched him to the soul. There was a depth of feeling that betrayed a heart that had been crushed. Long after Waffon had gone on deck, did Alfred stand by the mate's side and hold his weakening hand.

"Did he not say I should live three days?"

"He said a few days."

"Yes, that will do; but I shall never see Old England again. Alfred, you may be wanted on deck."

"But you may want something."

"No, not at present. Go on deck now. I shall live a few days; but before I die, I shall have something for you."

"For me?"

"——sh! Breathe not a word to another ear! Yes, for you. Who is that?"

Alfred turned his head and saw the captain.

"Ah, Mark, I'm sorry to see you laid out in this fashion!" said Pettrell, as he came down.

"It's fate, Marrok, fate! I may as well be laid out here, as anywhere. The world won't suffer at my loss."

Pettrell turned towards Alfred and motioned for him to leave the cabin. Our hero obeyed the silent order, and as he reached the deck he stopped a moment by the trunk, and he thought he heard Pettrell pronounce his name in an anxious tone. He stopped to listen. He could hear the hum of voices, and could hear that the subject of conversation was exciting to those engaged in it, but he caught no clue to its purport.

CHAPTER XIV.
THE DYING PIRATE'S REVELATION.

THE mainmast was secured alongside, and as soon as it was made safe, attention was turned to the burying of the dead. Twelve of the brig's crew had been killed, and three more, including Bronkon, had been wounded. The services of interment were very brief, and only a few moments elapsed from the time of preparation till the ocean's bosom closed over the corpse. There were no prayers, no funeral rites, only the bodies were sewed up in white hammocks and consigned to the grave of waters.

As soon as this had been done the men went to work again upon the floating mainmast. The rigging was got off and taken inboard; the top-gallant and topmast were got over, and then the lower mast was taken in, which was done by means of a pair of shears formed of spare spars. The lower mast was got in its place and very strongly fished and wedged, and before night on the following day, the brig was once more in sailing order, though much care was necessary that too much strain did not come upon the mainmast.

Pettrell was cross and crabbed, and he swore more than ever. For half an hour at a time he would pace the deck, speaking to no one, and hardly answering such questions as were put to him. The recent defeat had not only worried him, but he seemed moved by some other cause. The name of the wounded mate was often upon his lips, and at such times he would stop suddenly in his nervous walk and clasp his hands together.

It was the third day after the conflict with the American. Bronkon was worse, and Waffon had given him but a short time longer to live. Evening had set in and passed, and the first watch had been mustered. It was Pettrell's watch, but at an earnest request of the mate, Alfred was allowed to remain below.

Shortly after eight o'clock, Dunham came down and turned in, and ere long he slept soundly, for it was the first chance he had had since the battle.

"Alfred," said Bronkon, as he worked himself heavily over upon his side, "I am dying. I feel the icy hand upon my vitals."

"I hope you may die happy!" returned the youth.

"Ah, that is a vain wish!"

"Perhaps not. Heaven is not shut to him who sincerely repents."

"God knows I can repent!" uttered the dying pirate, with earnestness; "but Heaven cannot blot out the memory of the past. If there is a hell, Alfred, it must be imaged in the memory of a dying sinner. But my weakness is making me childish. The grim ghost of old death almost frightens me."

"Bronkon," said the youth reaching forth and taking one of the man's hands in his own, "you are not lost to every good feeling. You have still a soul, and if I am not in error, your early life has been poisoned by disappointment."

"S'death! who told you that?" uttered Bronkon, raising his head quickly from his pillow.

"No one but yourself. I have not failed to see that you have often crushed back good feelings that were rising in your bosom for utterance. I have seen the dark frown upon your brow grow darker when I knew it cost you an effort to make it so."

Bronkon's head settled back upon his pillow.

"You may be right," he said. "But enough of that. I have called for you to tell the story of my life, and when it is told, you will not wonder that I have looked upon you with strangely conflicting feelings. Are we safe from other ears?"

"Yes," returned Alfred.

"Then bend your head nearer. There. You will not breathe a word of what I may tell you to a soul on board of this brig?"

"No," said the youth, in a trembling tone.

Bronkon closed his eyes, and for a moment he writhed beneath the effects of the pain that worked along his nerves and muscles.

"Alfred," he said at length, in a low, trembling tone. "I have been at times most wretched; but I have suffered enough —suffered when no man knew it. I was not always wicked. My younger days were all joyous and happy, and plenty was mine. At an early age I saw a girl whom I loved. She was as beautiful as heaven itself, and I loved her as man may never love but once. I thought she returned my love, for she bore me company and seemed to enjoy my society. I was lost—utterly lost—in the heaven of my own love, and I dreamed not that a cloud could shut out my happy vision. But that cloud came. Another—a wealthier suitor— one of higher rank—came, and my idol turned from me. I begged, I implored— on my bended knees I besought the beloved girl to have compassion on me; but I found too late that she did not love as I had thought. She married my rival. Oh, what a sea of fire rolled over my heart then!"

Bronkon clasped his hands upon his bosom and groaned. It was pain that moved him, but it was bitter memory that made him weak enough to groan.

"You may never know such a keen torture as I then suffered," resumed the pirate. "It made me reckless and careless of life. But it was an unlucky hour for my soul when I fell in with Marrok Pettrell! A strange bond of sympathy found its way to our mutual knowledge, and we went forward on the path of revenge together. The man who had stolen away— no, no, I will not say that. It was not his fault that he loved her, for he knew nothing of me. But the man who had won my love for his bride, had incurred the sworn enmity of Pettrell, and he only sought for revenge. We had revenge, and it was dreadful! O God, forgive me! That was the most wicked act of all my life."

The speaker stopped and raised his hand to his brow.

"Alfred," he whispered, "you were the child of that woman I loved so wildly! ——sh! She now sleeps, and I shall see her in Heaven. Heaven! oh, if I should never reach it!"

"Great God! and was my mother"——

"——sh! I know what you would ask. She died soon after she gave you birth. Hers was a death that no mortal hand could have stayed. She sleeps beneath a marble slab in St. Margaret's yard at Westminster. There are marks of my tears upon that stone."

"Mark Bronkon, tell me of my father," uttered Alfred.

"I will give you more than you ask— more than you would dare to hope for—but I dare not have you know the whole story while you are with Pettrell. Alfred, I'm growing weak. There's drink in that cup."

The youth handed the cup to the dying man, and he placed it to his lips.

"Now reach your hand beneath my mattress," said Bronkon, as the cup was set back upon the table, "and you will feel a package. Give it to me."

The youth did as he was directed, and drew forth a package of papers. They felt like papers, but they were folded carefully in a piece of oiled silk, and tied with a piece of string. Bronkon took it.

"See if any one is near us," he said.

Alfred walked carefully to the foot of the ladder; but he found that no one was overhearing, and he returned to the pirate's side.

"In this package," said Bronkon, "there

is all concerning your father that you could wish to ask. Marrok Pettrell thinks these papers were burned long ago, but I burned a blank package in their stead, and these I have kept; for, strange as it may appear, I have long repented the deed I helped to consummate. When I last stood upon the spot where the mortal remains of her I loved were laid, I lost all my revenge; my heart softened in its bitterness, and I thought of doing justice to her son. When I give you this package, I shall have done all that lies in my power. I cannot restore to you all that you have been robbed of. Your father long since has passed away from earth, and he left behind him a son upon whose head rests the stigma of disgrace; but here is that which will clear your name from dishonor. If I give it to you, will you promise me that you will not open it while you are on board this brig?"

"If that be your request."

"It is my request; and you cannot have them otherwise. I will trust your honor."

"I pledge myself to obey you. But oh, tell me something of my father!"

"I can only tell you this: I saw his cold form given to the same grave that ere long will receive mine. I saw him buried, and I saw the blue waters close over him. There, ask me no more. Pass me the drink again; I am faint."

Bronkon took the can, but he had not the strength to hold it, and Alfred supported it to his lips.

"I do not taste it. It slips over my tongue without its usual flavor. Put it back. Raise my pillow, Alfred."

The youth raised the dying man's head, and he saw those dark eyes were fast losing their lustre.

"Put those papers in your bosom," feebly whispered the pirate. "Let not Pettrell see them, as you value your life. Ah, what was that?"

"I hear nothing," returned Alfred, bending nearer to the dying man.

"But I did. I hear the howl of the tempest. There! was not that a sea that broke over us? O God, what a dreadful cry was that! Some one is drowning. Alfred, hear the roar of the surge, and hear that wild cry again!"

Alfred could hear nothing save the dull rippling of the waves against the vessel's run, and the rattling of the cordage upon deck.

"Remember," whispered Bronkon, "open not those papers till you are clear of Marrok Pettrell. Hark! Who spoke to me then?"

"No one spoke," said Alfred.

"Yes—yes—I heard her voice!"

The pirate raised himself upon his elbow, and gazed fixedly into the face of the youth beside him, but his arm weakened, and he sank back.

"Do you feel much pain?" said Alfred.

There was no answer.

"Can I do anything for you?"

There was a slight motion of the head from side to side, but no answer.

Alfred reached forth and took the hand of the fallen man, but it was cold. He sprang to his feet and leaned over, but he heard no breath. The rays of the hanging-lamp fell upon the pirate's face, but they revealed features that had no expression. For a few moments he stood there and gazed into those dark features, and then he started from the strange thoughts that were crowding upon him, and he laid his hand upon the storm-beaten brow of the pirate, and whispered a simple prayer. Then Alfred drew the blankets smoothly over the motionless form, and and having felt in his bosom to see that the package was safe, he hurried on deck to tell the captain that Mark Bronkon was dead.

CHAPTER XV.

THE STORM-AVENGER.

ALFRED stood by and saw the corpse of the pirate mate consigned to the ocean, and as he turned away from the scene, his soul was the seat of strange emotions. He was soon aroused from his reverie by the weight of a hand upon his shoulder, and on turning, he met the gaze of Pettrell.

"What sort of a story did Mark Bronkon tell, before he died?" asked the pirate captain, in a low tone.

"Nothing," quickly returned Alfred; for he hesitated not an instant at the thought of deceiving the base wretch who was seeking his ruin.

"Something! He told you something," said Pettrell, while he sought to read the very thought-marks upon the youth's face.

"So he did. He told me of his suffering and approaching death."

"Don't attempt to deceive me. He told you more than that. Just tell me what has given your face that strange look of anxious concern since last night? What has made you cast such searching, meaning glances at me? By heaven, there's something in the wind! Now out with it!"

"I will tell you what I have thought, Marrok Pettrell. I have thought of the fearful price you have paid for the cargo you now have on board. Seventeen human souls!"

"Ah!"

"Yes. And I have thought, too, that those souls are but the first instalment upon a still more fearful retribution."

"Stuff!"

"No, no, Pettrell, you cannot so easily hide the truth from your soul. Let me tell you one other thing that has held a place in my thoughts."

"Silence!"

"Let me speak but this: I have thought that you dared not look far into the future. You may dwell as you please upon the past, and revel recklessly in the wild passions of your present career, but you cannot, without trembling, look forward to that which is to come. Do I not speak the truth?"

"No. You lie!" gasped the pirate captain.

"Then my thoughts, since the death of Mark Bronkon, have only reached to a lie," calmly, but emphatically, returned Alfred.

"Now you lie again! Mark Bronkon blabbed something to you; but little good will it do you."

Marrok Pettrell was in a rage when he turned away. How much he might have suspected Alfred could not judge, but the young man felt that his secret was safe, and he had no fear that the evil man could wrest it from him.

It was evident that the ardor of the crew had been dampened by the late catastrophe, and in the loss of the mate they felt that they had lost their best man. Yet they were ripe for evil as ever, and they stood ready to retrieve their fortunes by any means that might present itself.

On the fifth day after the death of Bronkon, a sail was reported to the southward, nearly in the pirate's wake; but Pettrell had no thought of turning from his course. At night the sail was lost to sight, and on the following morning it was not to be seen. Several times during the three succeeding days, the same sail, or one precisely similar, was seen in the same direction.

On the morning of the tenth day, when the light of the rising sun beamed over the waters, the strange ship was made out astern, and her heavy courses could be seen. Waffon was seen aloft with the glass, and at the end of five minutes he came back again, his face pale with excitement.

"It's a sloop-of-war!" he said, as he reached the quarter-deck.

Marrok Pettrell started forward and caught the glass, and then sprang up the main-rigging.

"It's a sloop-of-war!" he uttered, when he returned to the deck.

"Then she must have been lying in Teneriffe when that American ship went in," said Dunham.

"Yes, and she is now after us," added Pettrell.

The men gathered aft with anxious faces, for they had heard the report, and they seemed to be aware of the danger of their situation.

"If she has seen us," said Waffon, "there is no such thing as running away from her."

"By the great heavens, we must run away!" uttered Pettrell. "The coast of Old England will be in sight in a few hours, at least; and if nothing else can save us, we must take our money and make the best landing we can. The mainmast must stand her full sails. Get up the larboard stun'-sails, sir, and have them set."

Waffon urged that the mast would not bear it, but he was overruled, and the sails were set. The wind was fresh from the southward and westward, and as the mainmast felt the force of the new power, it bent and creaked beneath the load.

"She'll never bear it," uttered Waffon.

"She must bear it," was Pettrell's laconic reply, as he levelled his glass upon the ship. "By my soul, we can hold our own with her now. If we can but stand on clear of her guns till night we are safe."

"Land ho!" came at this moment from the foretopmast cross-trees.

"Where away?" cried the captain, starting forward.

"Three points on the lee bow," replied the man aloft.

"The Scilly Islands," said Pettrell. "Foretop, there! Can you make out a beacon?"

"Think I can."

"That's St. Agnes. By heavens, Waffon, we shall pass the islands by noon, and before night we shall be well up on the Cornwall coast. We'll give that war-dog the slip yet."

The crew were somewhat re-assured by the manner of the captain, and they cheerfully turned their whole energies to the working of the brig. It was soon evident that the sloop-of-war was not gaining—or at least not enough to be perceptible. She still maintained about the same distance. The heads of her courses were in sight, and from the tops a heavy swell would ever and anon give a view of her bulwarks.

Early in the afternoon the Scilly Islands had been left upon the starboard quarter, and then the brig's head was put towards the coast of Cornwall. At length the intervening islands shut the pursuing ship from sight, and the pirates began to count confidently upon their safety. Pettrell decided, after some consultation with Waffon and Dunham, to run for Barnstaple Bay, and make the mouth of the river Taw, if possible.

At three o'clock the log was thrown, and the brig was going ten knots strong.

"At this rate," said Pettrell, "we shall reach the bay by midnight. It is only about ninety-five miles. It will be nearly dark by the time the ship can see us again. Cheer up, cheer up, for we are safe yet."

"But this wind ain't agoin' to hold on so," said Waffon. "We'll have a change when the sun goes down."

"Then let it come," returned the captain. "We can stand it."

"Perhaps we can," murmured Waffon, half to himself, as he cast his eyes off towards the westward, where a low, dark cloud-bank rested upon the ocean. He did not speak all that he felt, for he would not give unnecessary alarm to the men; but he knew all the weather signs of those seas, and he saw an ominous one in the cloud-bank that arrested his attention.

Just before sundown the ship was made out again astern, but the attention of the crew was soon called from her by the lulling of the breeze.

"Look off there, cap'n," said Waffon, pointing to the west. "What does that look like?"

"It looks bad," said Pettrell, with a slight shudder.

Where the cloud-bank had lain, the horizon was changing to that color of bluish blackness which is more terrible in its look than the clear sable, and clear away off, as far as the eye could reach, little caps of white could be seen upon the wave-tops.

"We shall have it strong, sir," said Waffon.

"I believe you."

"A regular September gale."

"Yes," returned Pettrell. "But we must get the canvass off from our mainmast. By my soul, this is unlucky. Only six hours longer, and we might have been clear."

All haste was made to get the sail in, and soon the brig lay under close-reefed topsails and a storm staysail. By dark the gale was up in all its fury, and at length it was found necessary to bring the brig to the wind. In performing this evolution the lee fore-topsail parted and the sail was almost instantly snapped into ribbons.

"By heavens!" cried Pettrell, as he stood and saw the fore-topsail snapping in the wind, " if the main"——

His exclamation was cut short by the brig's being brought dead to the wind. Of course the main-topsail was taken aback. The vessel heaved and pitched, and just as Pettrell had given off orders to case the main-topsail sheet and clue up the sail, the heavy mainmast snapped its fishing, carried away its leading stays, and fell with a thundering, resistless crash over the stern.

For some time all hands were paralyzed with terror. Two men who were at the wheel were killed, and several more bruised. The mainmast was gone, and the fore-topsail was too far gone for use. The foresail could be of no use, for the brig could not lay to under it, as the heavy sea would keep the wind from it.

"How far are we from the shore?" said Dunham.

"Not over twelve miles," returned Pettrell.

"With a prospect of being nearer very fast," added Waffon.

"We must put the foresail on," said Dunham, " and try to lay along. That's the only thing we can do now."

Pettrell agreed to this proposition, and after the brig's head had been got off, the lee clue of the foresail was set; but it would not keep the wind, and in a few moments the ill-fated vessel was knocked off into the trough of the sea. Again did the despairing crew try to bring the brig to the wind, but all to no purpose.

"It's no use!" uttered the captain, as for the last time she refused to come up. "She must go as she will."

"Then we are lost!" broke from the lips of a dozen men.

"Only a miracle can save us," returned the captain, as he caught the rail for support.

"This may be the sum of the payment!" uttered Alfred.

Marrok Pettrell heard the remark, but he made no answer.

The sea was now breaking fearfully over the brig. All thoughts of making further efforts to save her had been relinquished, and the men were clinging to the racks and pins in utter despair. Alfred Harrold alone, of that whole crew looked upon the scene with calmness. There may have been a pallor on his face, a slight tremulousness in his nether lip, but he was not frightened. He looked forward to the coming crash that must wreck the brig as far more preferable than longer servitude with wickedness; and in his soul he could calmly say that death would not strike terror there.

Thus passed a long hour.

"Hark!" fell in stirring accents from the lips of one of the men.

"The coast!" uttered Waffon.

"Lost, lost!" groaned Pettrell.

Above the roar of the wind, and the lashing of the sea over the side of the pirate brig, could be heard the thundering of the distant surge, and some of the men, to whom such a thought had not occurred before for years, sank down upon their knees and uttered the name of their God in prayer! But they prayed too late! The hand of the avenger was upon them, and their hour of reckoning had come.

On dashed the brig, and louder grew the thunder of the surge. There was a grating of the brig's keel, a shock; then on again she dashed. Another grating, and another shock, another space of short moments, and then came the shock that fell with the death touch. The brig was hurled upon her side, and the mad sea tumbled wildly over her. Alfred felt the last trembling of the timbers beneath his feet, and his right hand was pressed upon his heart. He raised his eyes, and through the darkness he could see a mountain of water just towering above him. On it came. It broke—a wild cry sounded in his ears—his hold was broken, and with a single thought of heaven and his God, he was hurled into the boiling, surge beyond.

CHAPTER XVI.

FORE-SHADOWINGS.

ALFRED HARROLD came to himself, and he found that the sun was shining down on him. It was sometime ere he could command strength enough to raise himself upon his elbow, but he at length accomplished the undertaking. He found himself high up on a sandy beach, and half-buried in a great mass of sea-weed. His joints were stiff, but he was not long satisfying himself that no bones were broken, and that he was not seriously bruised. His right shoulder and hip were very lame, and the right side of his head he found to be somewhat sore. He had evidently struck amongst the sea-weed, and then was washed up on the beach.

It must have been nearly half an hour from the time our hero came to himself before he got upon his feet. The sea was still rolling in, but the gale had passed. It was a low beach where the brig had struck, but she had been completely knocked to pieces, and her cargo was scattered all around.

At some distance from the spot where Alfred stood were three men—poor fishermen, by their garb—who were hauling up a dead body from the wreck.

"Ah! you've come to, eh?" said one of the men, approaching our hero. "We thought there was life in ye. What a narrer 'scape you've had."

"It has been a narrow one," returned Alfred. "But tell me, who else is alive of the crew?"

"Don't know. There be three men as went off an hour ago. Guess all the rest be done for."

Alfred looked around among the bodies that were upon the sand. He found the stiff corpse of Waffon and Dunham, and fourteen more; but nowhere could he find Pettrell. He asked of the fishermen a description of the men who had gone.

"One on 'em was a real bruiser," said the man to whom the question had been put. "Had a great scar on his cheek, one on his nose, and I think one on his chin."

"Pettrell!" uttered Alfred.

"Yes, that be it. I heru t'other one call 'im so."

From further description, Alfred felt satisfied that one of the men named Paul Callum had also escaped; but the third he could not make out. The youth felt glad that Callum had escaped, for he had been his friend; and he was the one, too, who had taken the rope from Alfred's neck when Pettrell had thought to put his deadly threat into execution.

"So you be a smuggler, eh?" said one of the fishermen, with a peculiar wink.

"Yes, that is, this vessel was one," returned Alfred.

"Well, your capt'n needn't 'ave been so afeared, for there ben't nobody here as would harm 'im."

At this moment Alfred thought of the package he had received from Bronkon. He placed his hand in his bosom, but it was gone! For a moment he staggered beneath the blow; but coming to himself, he caught one of the fishermen by the arm.

"Who has robbed me?" he cried. "Who has taken a package from my bosom?"

"None of us hain't touched it," said the man.

"Them other fellers as went off felt around ye," said another; "and one on 'em picked up somethin' as looked like a paper."

"It was Pettrell," groaned our hero.

"Yes," said the fisherman.

"O God!" ejaculated Alfred, as the full sense of his loss came upon him; "he might have let me had that!"

"Money, eh?" uttered one of the men, with a sort of sympathizing look.

Alfred made no reply, but he turned to the spot from whence he had arisen and searched carefully in every direction; but he could find nothing of the lost package. It was gone, and the youth forgot for the time to thank God that his life had been saved.

"Come," said one of the fishermen, "you must be hurt an' hungry. Our home ben't fur from here. Come."

The youth did feel faint, and he refused not the man's offer. He gave one more search after the lost package, but without finding it, and then he followed the man up from the beach.

The fisherman's hut was only a few rods back from the head of the beach, and when our hero reached it he inquired in what part of Cornwall he was. He learned that he was about fifteen miles south of Stratton, and also that there were no neighbors within eight miles of the hut where he was, save a few more fishermen who had small cabins along the head of the shore.

A comfortable bed was provided for Alfred, and towards night he awoke from a refreshing sleep. Some decent cordial was procured for him, and one of the fishermen cooked him a palatable supper. Again he sought his bed, and it must have been nearly midnight when he was aroused by the sound of voices. He listened, and from such of the conversation as he could overhear, he learned that the three fishermen had found two boxes of the money which had been taken from the Indiaman.

Early on the following morning our hero arose from his bed greatly refreshed, and feeling quite strong. He partook of the plain fare that was set before him, and having finished his meal, he proposed to set forth.

"You ben't got no money, have ye?" asked one of the fishermen.

"No," returned Alfred.

The three fishermen whispered apart for a few moments, and then their spokesman turned to Alfred.

"Look ye," said he, with a curious expression upon his brown features. "I s'pose we may get somethin' out o' the stuff as was washed ashore, an' as part of it 'longs to you, why, yer see, we mout gin yer somethin'—say four gold guineas, eh?"

Alfred could almost have smiled at the fellow's manner, since he knew full well the secret of this generosity; but he betrayed no sign of his knowledge. At first he thought of refusing the money; but he knew that he might need it, and he accepted it.

"Now," said the man who had given him the money, "let me give you a piece of advice. There's been sharks arter yer, an' we set 'em on the wrong track. There's a sloop-o'-war come into Padstow yesterday, an' they're arter pirates. Some on 'em 'ave been up here, an' we set 'em off towards Camelford. Now you jes' take the fish-path right straight ahead to Stratton, an' from there you can go jes' as yer like."

"I am no pirate. I call God to witness that I am not," uttered Alfred.

"Well, p'raps ye ain't. But then if they think ye be, why, it's all the same, yer see; so yer'd better kind o' steer clear, ye know."

Alfred wished to say no more, so he thanked the fishermen for their kindness, and set off. He did not stop to look for the package he had lost, for he not only felt confident that Pettrell had got it, but he feared to make any stop. He was sure, from what the fishermen had told him, that the pirates had been traced to their wrecked vessel, and he trembled lest he should be arrested as one of them.

"Great God!" he mentally ejaculated, as this last thought occurred to him, "what a fate that would be!—to be arrested and dragged before the public as a pirate!"

The thought was terrible, and it presented a reality, too, which Alfred could not easily drive from sight. He almost felt that the black doom hung over him! He struggled, however, to overcome the fear, and he partially succeeded. He knew that he was innocent, and on that he rested his hopes.

The narrow road was easily made out, and before noon our hero reached Stratton. It was his aim to make the best of his way to the old light-house upon Little Devon Head. From Stratton to the north it was twelve miles to Hartland, and to this place the youth determined to make his way, only stopping in Stratton long enough to get a morsel to eat. The road was a mere cross-path along near the seashore; but it was easy, and before two o'clock in the afternoon the traveler reached Hartland, the most western town of Devonshire. Here he had the good fortune to find a stage bound to Barnstaple, a distance of twenty-eight miles; and in this

»tage, or, rather, on this stage, he secured a passage.

Alfred rode outside with the driver, the mail-guard being the only other outside passenger. The driver was an "old stager," and by dint of considerable perseverance he got Alfred into a conversation.

"Been to sea some, hain't ye?" he asked.

Alfred replied in the affirmative.

"Ever come across any o' them wagabond pirates?" resumed the driver.

The youth started, and for a moment his head swam; but his companion's attention was at that time directed to the horses, and he soon overcame his trepidation. The mail-guard was seated further up, so he did not notice the emotion.

"I have seen them," answered our hero.

"Blast 'em, I should like to see one on 'em. There's a cutter—a sloop-of-war's cutter, I b'lieve—come up to the pin't this mornin', and they said suthin' 'bout a pirate's brig bein' cast away on the coast somewhere. You heard anything about it?"

"Yes, I did hear something about it, but I took it to be only a rumor. By the way, that is a handsome horse—that starboard one forward. All four of them are very handsome ones, and, I doubt not, good ones."

"Good ones!" echoed the driver, giving his whip an extensive flourish, and drawing the reins tighter. "Good ones! Let me tell you 'at last Friday week I drove this team from Barnstaple to Exeter—an' that's hard on to forty miles"——

"Thirty-five," interrupted the mail-guard.

"Thirty-five be cussed!" retorted Jehu, not at all thankful for the matter-of-fact interruption. "But as I was sayin'—I drove this team from Barnstaple to Exeter—hard on to forty miles—in just four hours and forty-two minutes; an' I had to stop, too, at Dipford, an' Clumleigh, at Oldburrow, an' at the Silverton crossin' for passengers. That was this team."

Alfred expressed a due amount of wonder at this marvelous feat; and well he could afford to, since he had accomplished his object in drawing his companion's thoughts away from the pirates.

"Five-an'-thirty miles!" growled the old stager, as he flourished his whip with indignant emphasis. "These mail-guards thinks they knows everything."

After this our hero listened to any quantity of horse stories, and by flattering the peculiar vanity of the driver, he had risen wonderfully in the old fellow's esteem by the time the stage had reached Biddeford. Here two more passengers took outside seats, and from thence to Barnstaple Alfred had little occasion for conversation. It was nightfall when they reached their destination, and Alfred took lodgings at the tavern where the stage stopped. He had been somewhat acquainted in Barnstaple when he was with Luke Garron, and he had several times stopped at the very tavern where he now was; but no one recognized him, and as he had no desire to make himself known, he kept quietly in the back-ground, merely answering such questions as were casually asked him, and at an early hour he sought his bed.

At an early hour in the morning Alfred descended to the bar-room of the tavern, where he found quite a number of the town's people assembled, who were engaged in reading a placard that had been posted upon the wall. Our hero walked up to the spot, and found that the object of curiosity was no more or less than a full description of Marrok Pettrell, the pirate captain, and an offer of a large reward for his apprehension. The bulletin also stated that three others of the pirates had probably escaped, one of them a young man—and rewards were offered for them, too.

"Shouldn't think there'd be much trouble in making out that captain," remarked one of the lookers-on. "Zounds! what an ugly-looking customer he must be."

"I should know him the moment I put my eyes on him," said a second.

"Then there's t'others," added a third, "specially the young 'un. 'Gad, I'd like to make a haul on some on 'em."

Alfred felt his heart sinking within him.

It seemed to him as though all eyes must be fixed upon him, and he entertained at first the idea of leaving the place as quickly as possible; but he soon convinced himself that such a course would be the most likely to bring suspicion upon him, and with an inward struggle to overcome his trepidation, he walked calmly back towards the placard, and re-read it.

"Hallo," exclaimed a tammy-worker, who happened to cast his eyes upon our hero; "you be a sea-goin' chap?"

"Yes," returned Alfred, standing the simultaneous gaze of the crowd with unwonted fortitude.

"You ben't seen nothin' o' these pirates, I s'pose?"

"No, not I; and I pray that I never may."

The last part of this remark was made with a soul-fervor that might have disarmed suspicion had it ever existed.

"One o' them was a young 'un," remarked the tammy-maker; "but in course it couldn't 'a' been you?"

Alfred came nigh losing himself as this remark was made; but he saw that all eyes were upon him, and with a strong effort he maintained his composure.

"I shouldn't be very likely to be here if I were a pirate," said the youth, with a slight smile.

"No, in course not. But I hope as them fellers 'll be ketched—an' I hope as they'll be hung—an' I hope as I may be there to see 'em."

As the tammy-maker delivered himself of these hopes, he turned away to seek his place of business, and the rest of the people, one by one, gradually went their way.

Many a man loses a fortune by reaching too far for it, and many a one, too, fails to discover that of which he is in search, from the fact that the object is directly beneath his nose all the while. So it was with the people at the tavern. Had they found Alfred in the woods he would have been recognized as a pirate at once; but as it was, he was overlooked.

Our hero, however, could not feel easy

ALFRED READING THE OFFER OF REWARD FOR HIS APPREHENSION.

until he had got clear of the place; so as soon as he had swallowed his breakfast he set off. The road from Barnstaple to Comb Martin led directly north, and the distance was only eight miles; but Alfred chose to take a path directly to the Devon Head, which would be a distance of some sixteen miles. Part of the way was well traveled by footmen, and the whole way was easy. At length he crossed the small road that ran from Comb Martin to Parlock, and entered the oak woods beneath the shade of which he had so often gamboled when a boy, and ere long afterwards the little stone house and the beacon were in sight.

Near at hand were the three graves of the women who had been buried by the old light-keeper—and another had been added to the number. Its stone bore the name of "Nepsey." Alfred gazed in silence upon the grave, dropped a tear upon the cold sod, and then hurried on; but his heart was heavier, and a saddening misgiving had crept to his soul.

CHAPTER XVII.

THE NIGHT OF LIFE.

WITH trembling steps Alfred Harrold approached the home of his happy, joyous youth. At the door he stood for a moment irresolute, and then he knocked. It was a man who answered his call, but the man was a stranger. The youth hardly dared to ask his questions, but finally the name of the old light-keeper trembled upon his lips.

"So you're after Luke Garron, are ye?"

"Yes."

"Poor Luke!—he ain't here. But walk in."

The man returned to the keeping-room as he spoke, and with a tottering step Alfred followed him.

"Luke is not dead?" fell in a strained whisper from the youth's lips.

"Not as I knows on; but he hain't been here for over a year."

As the man answered, he looked inquisitively at his visitor, and gradually a beam of intelligence broke over his face.

"Perhaps," he said, "you are the boy that lived with him once?"

"Yes, he was a father to me. He saved me from the storm when I was a little child, and he"——

Alfred could go no further, for the thick-coming emotions choked him, and his eyes filled with tears. The man gazed sympathetically upon him, and he, too, was somewhat affected.

"Yes, yes," he said, "I heard all about it. Poor old Luke! He suffered a good deal after you had been taken from him."

"There was a girl with him—a beautiful young creature, whom he saved—or whom I saved—from the wreck of the 'Chesham.'"

"Ah, that was the trouble," returned the man. "Luke seemed to love that girl just as though she was his own flesh and blood, and when they come and took her away, it almost killed him. Nepsey had died before that, and he was left all alone."

"Took her away!" repeated Alfred. "Who did it?"

"Oh, it was her own father. You see he found out that Luke had found the girl, and when he came down here he knew her, so he took her away with him."

"Did you know the man?"

"No. Luke did not tell me who he was."

"And it might not have been her father, after all."

"Oh, yes it was, for Luke told me there was no mistake about it."

"And you know not where she has gone?"

"No."

"But Luke—you can tell me something of him?"

"I can't tell you where he is. All I know is, that he went away from here, and I was put in his place. Poor old man! He couldn't stay here after his storm daughter was gone. He always used to call her his 'storm daughter.' After you was gone it was bad enough; but after they came and took Ella away from him, he wasn't fit for business any more. He used to let the lamps go out dark nights, and then some-

THE STORM CHILDREN; OR, THE LIGHT-KEEPER OF THE CHANNEL. 53

times when there was a storm, he'd go and set out on the head of the bluff, and not light up the beacon at all. You see they couldn't have matters go on so, and they had to turn him off. I took his place, but it made my heart ache when I saw poor old Luke Garron go out from these doors. He was all broken down; that handsome form of his was bent, and his eye was dim; his hair was turned gray, and his brow was all furrowed and wrinkled. Poor Luke!"

Alfred bowed his head and wept like a child. His highest hopes of joy were crushed, and where he had looked for the returning sunshine of life, all was dark. He thought to see the dawning of day, but in the stead thereof he found it still night.

"Can you not tell me anything of Luke?" he asked, as he raised his head once more.

"Nothing since he went away from here," returned the light-keeper. "I haven't seen anything of him, nor heard anything."

It was a long time before Alfred spoke again, but he was at length aroused by the entrance of the light-keeper's wife. Dinner was prepared and the youth sat down to the same table from which he had eaten in childhood; but he could not eat much now. When the meal was finished, the light-keeper went up into the beacon to trim his lamps, and Alfred walked out upon the bluff.

Every spot, every rock, every twig, bore to the mind of the youth the memory of some happy scene. Here he had sat upon Luke's knee, and listened to that good man's counsels, and there he had played with the bright-eyed Ella. Then he was a playful, happy boy—now he had grown to be a man, and happiness had long been a stranger to his bosom. He went out upon the bluff, and looked off upon the broad bosom of the channel. Below him was the little sandy cove, shut in by its guardian rocks, and there lay the very boat he had helped Luke so often to manage. He turned to the narrow path and descended to the place. He entered the boat and sat down upon one of the thwarts, and then he buried his face in his hands. For nearly half an hour he sat there in one position, his mind busy in recalling the varied scenes of the past. Suddenly he felt a heavy hand upon his shoulder, and on starting to his feet he beheld the scarred and storm-beaten features of Marrok Pettrell.

"Eh! By the beard of Moses, but this is a lucky hit. Blow me eternally if I thought of seeing you here."

Alfred Harrold was thunder-struck. He gazed upon the pirate captain for some moments without the ability to speak.

"Lucky, by the powers!" said Pettrell. "But let's be off out of this. We'll work together now, and haul our wind quickly. Cut those gaskets, Alfred, and then give me a lift at the halyards. I'll cut the shore-fasts. Hurry, hurry, for the bloodhounds are after us. By my eternal soul, if we can get out of this lugger, we may laugh at them."

"You may go your own way, Marrok Pettrell, but I shall keep your company no longer."

"Nonsense! I tell you the officers are almost here! They gave me chase on the road, and I took to the woods; but they found my wake. Come, bear a hand, and let's be out of this."

"You can go, but I shall not go with you."

"Fool! dolt! Would you be taken by the hounds?"

"I am no pirate."

"Ha, ha, ha! You may tell them that story, but they won't believe you."

"You know, Marrok, that I am not."

"No, I don't know any such thing."

"Good God! you wouldn't see me taken."

"Oh, shut up your nonsense!" hastily exclaimed Pettrell, as he drew a knife across the gasket of the sail. "We've sailed together too long to part company now. If I am taken, you'll be taken with me; and what is more, if I'm hanged, you'll be hanged with me. Now you'd better start up and help me off."

The youth for a moment was astounded by the cool villany of the pirate, but he soon regained his firmness and decision.

"Go your own way, Pettrell," he said; "but think not that I shall go with you. I have little choice between your company and that of the officers."

"Fool!"

"Ah!" uttered Alfred at that moment, thinking of the package he had lost, "you robbed me of papers that I had."

"Papers? What papers?" exclaimed the pirate in assumed astonishment.

"You took them from my bosom while I lay"——

"I know nothing of papers. Ha! did Mark Bronkon give you papers?" cried Pettrell, seizing the youth by the arm. "Tell me!—tell me! Did he give you any papers?"

Alfred now believed that Pettrell had not taken those papers, for there was surely no deception in his earnest, anxious manner; but before he could reply, the pirate dropped his arm and sprang to the shore-fast.

"They are upon us!" he cried. "Out with that boat-hook! Out with it—quick! For mercy-sake, Alfred, help me to escape!"

The shore-fasts were cut, and Alfred attempted to leap to the shore, but Pettrell seized hold of him and held him back.

"By heavens, you shall not leave me! You must help me now. Hear them? They are at the house and will soon be here! Seize those halyards!"

"Marrok Pettrell," exclaimed the youth, shaking off the hold that was laid upon him, "I have said that I will no longer be your companion. I mean that, and by that will I abide."

"Back! Move a step towards the shore, and you shall die!"

As the pirate spoke, he seized the boat-hook and attempted to push off; but his efforts were in vain, for the boat's keel was bedded in the sand. He turned to seek the assistance of the youth, and at that moment half-a-dozen men appeared upon the head of the bluff.

"O fool! Infernal, dastard fool!—we are lost!" cried Pettrell, as he gave one more desperate push with the boat-hook.

He pushed in vain, and in a moment more the officers leaped on board the boat. The stout pirate made a strong resistance, but he was soon overpowered by numbers, and his arms pinioned behind him.

"Now whom have we here?" asked the leader of the officers, as his eyes rested upon our hero.

"That is one of them," said an officer.

"Who are you?" asked the leader.

"I am no pirate, sir—God knows I am not!" uttered Alfred.

"Then God must have a curious way of knowing things," said Pettrell, with a demoniac look.

"There was a young one among them," said one of the officers, "and it's likely that this ere is him."

"Didn't you belong on board the brig that was wrecked on the Cornwall coast?" asked the leader.

"Yes, I did," groaned Alfred; "but I was"——

"Oh, never mind your buts," interrupted the officer. "I expect to hear this chop-faced villain swear that he ain't a pirate next."

"He's the one; but he is a little frightened," said another of the officers.

Alfred offered no resistance, for he knew that it would be useless; neither could he say any more, for he was only met with coarse taunts, and with a painfully swelling heart he was led up from the cove.

"The light-keeper came out, and saw the prisoners led by the house. Alfred could see the wonder that rested upon his countenance, but he had no word to say. It was a crushing blow, and he sank beneath it. Silently he walked along through the woody path, and at the road he found horses. Upon the back of one he was secured, while Pettrell was in like manner secured upon another. The officers then mounted, and the party set off towards Exeter, which place was reached late in the evening.

Here Alfred and Pettrell were lodged in the jail, but in different cells, and at the end of a month they were forwarded to London, to answer to the charge of piracy.

When our hero reached the great metropolis, he was sick at heart, and all worn down with grief and misery. All along upon the road he had been gazed at as a felon of the blackest dye, and on more than one occasion had been forcibly assaulted by the mob. At length the prison doors were shut upon him at London, and he knew that when he came forth it would be to his final trial. He knew of no means to secure a witness in his behalf, unless, indeed, he might gain something from the influence of Sir William Brent. He remembered, too, his address. He received permission to write a note to the old admiral, and he did so, and sent it off. He waited two weeks, but he heard nothing from his letter. Marrok Pettrell had sworn to claim the youth as a pirate, and there seemed no earthly way for redemption.

The most fearful ordeal of his whole eventful life was now before the unfortunate youth. He feared that the Court of the King's Commissioner would condemn him. But one ray of light still shone in upon him: at the bar of God he knew that he would be innocent.

CHAPTER XVIII.

THE TRIAL.

THE day of trial at length came, and Alfred Harrold was taken to the court where he was to be tried for his life. The ship which had been robbed in the Indian Ocean had arrived in port, and many of her passengers were there as witnesses.

The great hall was crowded with spectators, and the utmost interest prevailed. Alfred met the eager gaze of the people as he entered the box, but as soon as he could be seated, he bowed his head and covered his face with his hands.

By previous arrangement Pettrell and the youth were tried separately. With the pirate captain the case was a short and direct one. Ten men who had been on board the Indiaman knew him on the instant they saw him, and their testimony was direct and conclusive. He was found guilty of piracy, and the judge asked him if he had any reason to give why the sentence should not be pronounced upon him. Pettrell arose to his feet, and cast a defiant look around upon those who had collected there to look upon him.

"Yes, your honor," he said, with a cool look and tone, "I suppose my case is a fixed one, and the idea of asking a man his reasons for not being hanged, when you have determined to hang him at all events, is a novel idea. However, my time has come. You want my life. Take it. I suppose my companion here will follow in the same track. He hasn't been quite so long an outlaw as I have, but that is his lookout. I could almost wish that he hadn't been caught, for he is too young to hang. If he should live he might repent; but then your laws don't look at such things. We both must die. No, sir, I have no reason why I should not be hanged. I have played the game and beat it often; now I'm beat. If I have any complaint to make, it is that you should put us on separate indictments. Alfred and myself have been together, and the same testimony that applies to me will apply to him. He is my son, 'tis true, but"——

"Liar!" uttered a voice in the crowd.

The judge commanded order.

"Excuse me, your honor; but that base wretch's words are having weight against one who is yet to be tried. He has lied most foully."

All eyes were turned in the direction from whence the voice proceeded, and Sir William Brent, the admiral of a hundred battles, was seen making his way towards the bench.

"Your honor!" he exclaimed, his white locks shaking with the indignation that moved him, "I know that youth, and I knew his father. Let the dastard villain speak no more."

Marrok Pettrell trembled for a moment, and then he stamped his foot with rage. He was paralyzed for awhile, but his reckless daring came back to him.

"Let me tell the admiral that he is too late to triumph!" hissed the pirate, with a fiendish look. "He and I looked on and saw a man hanged years ago. If this young pirate by my side is not my son, much good it may do when he finds out in reality who was his father. I am now ready for your hangman!"

A ray of hope had shot through our hero's soul when he heard the old baronet, but a strange source of new grief was opened to him by the last words of Pettrell. He had heard Bronkon speak of his father being buried at sea, and he remembered Bronkon's manner when the subject was broached. The thought came like a thunderbolt upon him that his father had been hanged! And then came the thought of the papers he had lost.

Sir William conversed a moment with the clerk of the court, and then he whispered with the judge; and soon afterward sentence of death was passed upon the pirate captain, and then the officers were ordered to remove him from the room. Pettrell objected to this; but his objection was of no avail, and with a volley of oaths upon his lips he was led from the place.

It was now Alfred's turn to be called up. The appearance of Sir William had given him a glimmer of hope; but yet the evidence of the ship's passengers was somewhat against him, until one was called who had seen the pirate captain knock him down. Four of the passengers were confident they had recognized the youth upon the quarter-deck of the pirate brig, but they all agreed that he did not board the ship. The fifth witness stated that he saw Pettrell knock the prisoner down just as the brig began to round to.

After evidence for prosecution was all in, Alfred Harrold was requested to make any statement he chose bearing upon the question at issue.

"Nearly the whole of my life, sir, bears upon the terrible subject," tremblingly uttered the youth as he arose to his feet.

"Go on, the court will listen."

The youthful prisoner bowed his head for a moment, and then wiping the tears from his eyes, he cast a quick glance about him. He met the gaze of hundreds, but he saw that every countenance bore that magic beam of sympathy which is not to be mistaken; that beam which puts a brilliant spark in the eye, and a tender softness about the lips, which fastens the gaze with a kind look, and images hope in its expression. Quick as the passage of the lightning bolt went the conviction to the heart of our hero that the sympathy of the people was with him. This gave him courage, and with considerable firmness he commenced the story of his eventful life.

Alfred's voice trembled with emotion as he commenced; but gradually, he lost the realities of the present in the memories he was calling up. His tone assumed power, and the pathos of his words was deep and touching. With a modest, unwitting force, he painted the scenes of his early boyhood; he told how he had been saved from the wreck by the old light-keeper, and how he had lived with that good man, how he had learned, how he had loved, how his heart had put forth its tender shoots of hope, and how his life was opening in the summer of peace and joy. Then he told of the coming of the dark man who had just been taken from the court-room under the sentence of death.

For a moment the poor youth's feelings overpowered him, and he bowed his head on the railing before him. When he spoke again, his voice had settled to a low, painful cadence, and his frame trembled beneath the bitter memories he called up. With living, speaking colors he painted the night of storm and darkness that shut so fearfully about him when he was dragged away from his kind protector, and as he went on with his recital every eye that beamed upon him was moistened with the warm dew of generous sympathy. He told of his dark sorrows, and his soul's battle against the evil genius that had settled down so menacingly by his side. He told of his escape from the brig in Cumberland, of his meeting with Sir William Brent, and of his subsequent re-capture.

And so he went on, giving a faithful picture of his career up to the time of the wreck upon the coast of Cornwall. His tears flowed afresh as he told of the bitter disappointment he had experienced when he had reached once more the home of his boyhood, and how, at that moment, his life's hopes were again crushed. Then he told how the pirate captain had again met him, and how once more his fate seemed linked with that of the dreaded man who had been his deadly enemy so long. There was a moment's pause, and then Alfred raised his clasped hands towards heaven, and while his countenance beamed with a holy radiance, he exclaimed:—

"Earth can have few joys left for me now; but, oh, I would not have my name left upon her history linked with a crime so black. God knows my heart; to him I can look as a child may look up to a father. He will have mercy on the unfortunate, and soothe the troubles of those who rest upon his arm. To my God I am not afraid to commit myself: to my fellows, and to you, sir, I look for pity, at least; pity for one who has been most bitterly wronged, and whose heart is all crushed and broken.

Some minutes elapsed after the youth had sank into his seat, before a whisper broke the stillness that reigned in that room. When it was broken, it was by a low, simultaneous heaving of a hundred bosoms that sent forth the pent-up emotions of unmistakable good-will and sympathy.

Sir William Brent arose at the call of the clerk, and gave his testimony.

"Sir William," said the judge, after the old admiral had related the circumstances of his meeting with the youth in Cumberland, "you know something, I think, of the prisoner's early life?"

"Nothing that I may tell here, my lord," returned the old man. "It can have no bearing upon the prisoner's case."

In a short time the case was given to the jury, and after a deliberation of some minutes they returned with a verdict of "Not guilty."

The feelings of the excited multitude were not to be restrained, and they burst forth in a prolonged shout of applause, in the midst of which Alfred sank back completely overpowered. He heard the shout, and he knew that he was safe, and then his consciousness left him. When he was aroused, his hand was clasped by a warm embrace, and a friendly voice was speaking to him.

"Come, come, my brave youth; you are free!"

It was Sir William who spoke to him, and as our hero caught the kind look of the old man's eye, he bent forward and leaned his head upon the baronet's bosom.

"Come, come; you are free!"

"But whither—whither shall I go?"

"With me," returned the baronet, as he led the youth from the box. "Come; my carriage is in the street."

Alfred followed the old man out, and as he walked down the aisle he met the warm greetings of those who had remained to see him depart. He thanked them with a silent, tearful look of gratitude, and ere long he reached the admiral's carriage. Once more he turned his grateful look upon the multitude who were cheering him, and then he entered the vehicle of his friend. He knew not why the old man should be so interested in him; but of one thing he felt assured—that Sir William was his friend, and that for the present he was safe from persecution.

CHAPTER XIX.

A STRANGE SURPRISE.

It was nearly dark when Alfred reached the residence of Sir William in Hanover Street. He ascended the steps and followed the admiral into the hall, where he waited till one of the servants had called the secretary.

"Mr. McIvar," said the old gentleman, "I wish you to take this young gentleman with you to Walbourne's and there see that he has clothing suitable for a guest of mine. He is the one of whom I have often spoken. You know him?"

"Yes," returned the secretary, as he cast a kind look upon the youth.

Our hero could not object to this arrangement, and with a word of thanks upon his lips, he followed McIvar back to the carriage, and they proceeded at once to Walbourne's. The fashionable tailor had any quantity of superb clothing on hand which had never been called for by those who had ordered it, and without difficulty Alfred was fitted with a suit. As he surveyed his counterfeit in a mirror, he could not but feel a thrill of new pleasure; for, say what we will, outward appearance is not to be overlooked in this world of ours. Dress may not "make the man;" but dress does make the man of fine feelings more agreeable to himself, and more pleasing to others. Labor has her garb of "stout contents," and labor is honorable in that garb; but the hand that sweats in the dust of toil should not go unwashed to the tea-table. Neatness and comeliness have their laws, and to a certain extent even fashion may be just.

When Alfred returned to the dwelling of Sir William, he was shown into a large drawing-room, where he was told that the admiral would soon join him. For a little time the youth was completely dazzled by the gorgeousness of things about him. The large shaded lamps sent a soft light around upon the rich carpets, and the heavy, carved furniture, and the old pictures that looked forth from their gilded frames seemed like tiny spots of nature in the distance, seen through golden windows.

A portrait that hung against the wall opposite to the door, had just attracted the youth's attention, and he was so deeply buried in the contemplation of the beautiful features which were there revealed, that he did not notice the opening of the door, nor the sound of a light footfall that approached him; nor was he aroused till he felt a hand upon his shoulder, and heard a low, sweet voice pronounce his name.

He started to his feet, and, as he turned, his eyes rested upon a face of more than ideal beauty and loveliness. The lips upon which he gazed were half parted, and a gentle smile was breaking about them.

"Ella!" he whispered, half fearful that his dream was false. "Ella!"

"Your own little storm child," returned the fair girl.

Both her hands were extended as she spoke, and her eyes were fixed with a beaming look upon the face of the youth. He thought not then of the maiden who stood before him with the first dawn of blushing womanhood upon her cheeks; he only thought of the little child he had wrested from the storm grasp, of the gentle being who had been his companion in the flowery walks of boyhood, and of her who had been the love light of many a dark hour of tempest and tribulation. With these thoughts, these feelings, he drew the beautiful Ella to his bosom, and pressed his lips upon her fair cheek.

"And you, too, here," he murmured, as he again gazed into Ella's face. "Has Sir William been kind to us both?"

"Ah, Alfred, I have found a father in Sir William."

"Father!" uttered the youth, dropping the hands he held, while a sudden shade of something like fear passed over his features.

"Yes, and a good, generous father he is," said Ella, with a happy look.

"Thank God for the blessing he has conferred upon you!" ejaculated the youth, as he sank back into his seat.

The beautiful girl sat down by his side, all unconscious of the sudden pang that found its way to Alfred's heart. She knew not that in her present sphere her companion felt that she was removed from him forever.

But so it was. He had held the sweet companion of his boyhood in his soul's memory for years, and he had learned to look upon that image as the type of one who belonged to him in love and sympathy. But the scene was changed. The child he had taken to his young bosom from the grasp of death, was no longer a traveler in the same path with himself, and he felt that henceforth she could only be his companion in the memory of days that had passed. But the youth hushed the feelings that were rising in his bosom, and once more he turned with a smile to the fair being at his side.

"Ella," he asked, "have you seen anything of our old protector since you left the beacon house?"

"Once I thought I saw him," returned the girl, while an expression of sadness overshadowed her features. "I stood by the window and saw an old man upon the opposite side of the square. It looked like old Luke, and I ran out to meet him, but when I had gained the street he was gone. I have seen nothing of him since, nor have I heard anything of him."

At this moment Sir William entered the apartment, and Alfred quickly arose to meet him.

"Ah, you look like another man, upon my soul," exclaimed the old man, as he took our hero's hand. "What do you think of the surprise you have met?"

"It was a heavenly surprise, sir," returned Alfred.

"I thought so. My pretty Ella must seem a very sister to you."

"Yes," said the youth in a low tone, while his eyes wandered to where the fair girl sat.

"I knew she must; and it seems, too, that you were the one who saved her."

"Yes. I took her from the cold bosom of one who clung to her even in death. I think she would have died had I not discovered her as I did."

"And God knows you shall ever have my warmest gratitude—and something substantial, too. But has Ella told you the story of her early life?"

"No, sir."

"Then you are yet in the dark. But I will explain the matter. Let's see—it is thirteen years ago that her mother died. How time flies away. I then had command of a squadron in the Indies. My wife was taken with one of those malignant fevers, and she died in one week from the time of her first sickness. She left my Ella not quite four years of age, and I at once made up my mind to send the child to England. I wrote letters to my friends in London, with whom I had planned that Ella should remain till I came home, and gave them into the hands of the captain of the ship in which my child was to sail. The child's nurse, and two more of my female servants, were sent to take charge of my little daughter. Of course the letters never reached their destination, and when the old light-keeper sent word out that he had found a child—as I understand he did—there was no one in England who mistrusted that my child had left the Indies.

"When I came home, which was nearly two years afterwards, I thought my child had perished. The account of the wreck of the "Chesham" reached me in Calcutta, and that gave out that every soul on board the ship perished. Not a thought entered my head that my child could have been saved, and I gave her up as lost. Seven years passed away after my return, and during that time I divided my attention between my friends in London and my estates in Cumberland. You remember our meeting at the little inn near Egremont? When you told me your story then, you said something about a girl who had been saved. My then present interest in other matters prevented me from noticing the circumstance; but ere long after I set out on the road your words came back to my mind, and by degrees the idea of my own child became associated with the little girl of whom you had spoken.

"When I returned to London, I hastened off to Devonshire. I found the residence of the old light-keeper—and there I found my daughter. She had grown to be a large girl, but I knew her the moment I saw her. She had retained her Christian name—Ella Deane—for that was what we always called her, though she had forgotten the name of her family. The facts were as clear as though my child had never been absent from me for a moment; but it gave me a pang to take her away from that old man. He wept like a child, and I thought his heart would break. I asked him to come and live with me, but he refused. He said he had nothing on earth to live for, and I believe he spoke the truth. It was a heavy blow for him. Ah, Ella—does it affect you so?"

"Excuse me, my dear father," said the fair girl, as she wiped the tears from her face. "Alas, poor Luke! I cannot think of him but with sorrow. He was a good man. He was a father to me when I had none else to protect me, and I shall ever love him! Alas, poor Luke! what would I not give to see him?"

"But tell me, Sir William," uttered Alfred, struggling to keep back his tears, "do you not know anything of that old man now?"

"No. He left the light-house shortly after I took Ella home, and I have heard nothing of him since. I have sent to Devonshire repeatedly, but could gain no clew to his whereabouts."

Gradually the conversation took another turn, though it was a long time ere Alfred could draw his thoughts from the unfortunate protector of his boyhood. At length, however, he overcame the sadness that loaded his soul, and then he had to recount the scenes of his own life. He had an interested listener in Ella, and often did he feel the warm blood rushing to his face as he met the earnest expression of her lustrous eyes.

It was late when Alfred was shown to his chamber, and when he was once more alone, what a rushing of various emotions filled his bosom. Into that one day were crowded the prison—the court—the trial—the host of applauding people—the unexpected protector—and last, the meeting with Ella. It is no wonder that it was long ere he slept, nor is it a wonder that when he did sleep his dreams were various and wild. If he dreamed of Ella, it was as one might dream of airy castles which had substance only in vain wishes.

CHAPTER XX.

THE HEART'S SECRETS, AND ITS TRIALS.

ON the very next morning after Alfred had found protection beneath the roof of Sir William Brent, the latter received orders to go to Portsmouth to attend a court-martial. The call was an urgent one, and the old admiral had to obey it. His secretary was to attend him, and our hero was to be left almost alone with Ella.

"You can make yourself comfortable till my return," said Sir William, speaking to the youth, just previous to his departure. "There is my library, and if you at any time wish to take a ride, the coachman will obey your wishes. I shall be absent two weeks, at least, and perhaps three; but when I return I will attend to your interests. However, a few weeks of rest will not harm you. And you, my child," continued the baronet, turning to Ella, "will of course do everything in your power to make Alfred comfortable. You owe him a debt of deep gratitude, and you must not forget that I owe him the life of my child."

Sir William set off, and the storm children were once more left to enjoy each other's society. For a week there was a mutual constraint. They conversed and read together, but their conversation was formal, and the reading was resorted to for the purpose of relieving the tedium. Both those hearts were swelling with thoughts and feelings for which there had been no utterance, except by the soft language of those tones and glances which could not be restrained. Alfred told over and over again the tale of his trials and sufferings upon the sea; and often were the scenes of those days, when both were children under the care of the old light-keeper, reverted to and talked about.

During the second week, Alfred opened his heart more to the feelings that lay so closely about it, and he smiled oftener, and spoke more freely. The effect was not lost upon Ella, for her very joyous looks told how happy she was, and how much she loved the society of him who had thus been left to bear her company.

The third week had opened, and Sir William had not returned. Alfred and Ella were sitting in the baronet's library. It was evening, and they had been conversing upon topics connected with their childhood. They were seated upon the same soft lounge, and they had been more than usually thoughtful.

"Oh," uttered Ella, "I shall never tire

in looking back upon those sweet scenes of my early childhood."

"We were happy, then," said Alfred.

"Yes, and we are happy now."

"Happy in the present, Ella; but there is a future."

"And there must be happiness there, too," said the fair girl.

"Perhaps so," returned Alfred, gazing half sadly into the face of his companion. Their eyes met. Over the face of Ella there came a strange look of unmistakable love, and gently she put forth her hand and rested it upon Alfred's arm.

"Tell me your thoughts," she said.

"They are such as may not be spoken," returned the young man, while his nether lip trembled.

"Then they were not of me?"

"Of you?"

"If you would not speak them, how can they be?"

"Ah, Ella—they are of you."

"Then speak them."

"Would indeed I dared."

The fair girl started and gazed more earnestly into her companion's face. She saw the trembling of the lips, and she saw, too, the glittering tear that stood upon his dark lashes. She moved her hand closer to his own, and soon it was nestled there.

"Tell me, Alfred," she whispered, while her heart fluttered till its beatings were almost audible, "the thoughts that move you thus."

"Can you not read them?"

"Yes."

"Then why should I tell them?"

"They might be music to my soul."

"Ella!"

"Can you not understand me, Alfred?"

"Oh, I cannot be mistaken," exclaimed our hero. "You do know my heart, and you can return me the warmest feelings of your own. You have unloosed my tongue, and I will speak. I love you, Ella, with my whole soul I love you."

"And of that you were thinking?"

"Yes, and of that I have thought since I came beneath this roof."

"And are you not happy in that love?"

"Happy?"

"Ay, Alfred—happy? You used to be happy when you loved me."

"Yes, yes; but 'twas not such love as this. Then I felt you were all my own, and the affections of my young heart clung about you to protect and shield you. Now you no longer need my protection. We are grown up, and the sentiments we cultivate will be firmly fixed in our fates. I cannot hide it from me that my love would be dangerous now."

"Dangerous?" repeated Ella, with a startled air.

"Ay!"

"I do not surely understand you."

"You can see it all, Ella; but yet I can speak more plainly."

"Speak," the fair girl whispered.

"Then since you bid me, you will know my heart. I have told you that I love you; but, oh, mine is a love that must not be cherished unless it may live in the presence of its object evermore. In short, there is one holy name that can alone give forth its image; one name alone on all the earth that can syllable its thought."

"And that name?" murmured Ella.

"Wife," uttered Alfred in a thrilling tone.

Ella bowed her head, and her hand trembled violently. But soon her eyes were fixed again upon her companion, and a fond, affectionate smile was breaking around her finely chiselled lips."

"Alfred," she said, with only a slight tremulousness in her tone, "you have told me that which I had fondly hoped might be true."

"But can there be hope for me?"

"Why should there not be? Your heart can feel no more than can mine. Ah! Alfred, you little know me, if you think I could forget all those tender sympathies and gentle deeds of kindness that were the sunbeams of my girlhood. No, no, my heart is all your own—all—all"——

"O God bless you, sweet Ella!" ejaculated the youth, as he pressed the fair girl to his bosom.

Their lips met, and with that simple kiss was locked the chain that mortal hand might never put asunder.

Moments passed; bliss-laden moments, ere Alfred spoke again. Then a cloud settled over his features, and his deep blue eye looked sad.

"Ah! I knew you loved me," he said; "but there is a third whose will must be law, that shall govern our fates. Your father's wishes may not be in my favor."

"O Alfred, you wrong my father, if you think he would oppose us in our love. He is too generous, too kind, too noble-hearted for that."

"I know he is kind and generous; but I fear you misunderstand him."

"Ah, no! It is you who misunderstand him, Alfred. He would not have left us here together, had he entertained objections to our union. What do I not owe you?" she continued, with increased warmth. "What does he not owe you? I know Sir William will not oppose us. He will not crush the holiest blossom of my whole opening womanhood."

And so the sanguine girl thought. She looked upon her companion with the whole loving confidence of her ardent soul, and she knew not that earth had an obstacle to throw in the way of her hopes. But with Alfred the case was different. His life had been one of disappointment, and even now he could not shake off the heavy load of fear that weighed him down.

"Come, come," said Ella, as she noticed the deepening sorrow on her lover's face; "be happy as you used to in years gone by. We will be as we were then, and through our whole life we shall remain so. You shall love me and care for me, and I will share your every sorrow, and never, never cease to love you. Come, be happy now, and smile as you used to smile."

"Blessed, blessed girl!" cried Alfred, while the warm tears started forth from his eyes. "You will make me hope in spite of myself."

"No, no, you shall hope with a hope that hath foundation. Love shall bid you hope; and love is a gentle, yet powerful monitor."

"Oh, would that I could throw every doubt away. Would that I could see the future as bright as your love's pencil paints it."

"Hark! O Alfred, that is my father's step. Some time you shall ask him all. You will, and I will be your second. He will not refuse us."

Alfred opened a book that lay by his side, and while he was yet endeavoring to remove the tear marks from his face, the old admiral entered. Ella sprang to meet him. He kissed her fair brow, and then he turned to Alfred.

"Home once more," he said, as he grasped the young man by the hand. "Ah! we had some bad business at Portsmouth. There's to be a hanging at the end of our work."

Alfred trembled like an aspen, and then his face turned pale as death. Sir William then for the first time noticed the youth's tears. A dark shadow flitted across his own face, and for some moments he gazed fixedly into the features of his young guest.

"Ella," he said, turning to his child, and seeming to speak more for the purpose of saying something behind which to hide his real thoughts than to convey any news of importance, "we shall have company tomorrow. My old friend, Doctor Holland, came on with me from Portsmouth. He was my surgeon for many years; and as for you, Alfred, I think that between the doctor and myself we can bring about a good berth for you."

The young man expressed his gratitude, and shortly afterwards he arose and left the room. A thought had entered his mind that made his head reel with wild emotion, and he only sought to be alone.

"Stop, Ella," said the old man, after Alfred had gone, "I wish to speak to you."

Ella stepped back to the seat from which she had risen, and her father continued:—

"What is the matter with Alfred?"

"Matter, father?"

"Yes. He had been weeping when I came in, had he not?"

Ella hesitated a moment, and then she arose and approached her father. She leaned over, and with her hand resting upon his arm, she said, in a tone of calm trust:—

"He had been weeping, father; but it was from fears that have no foundation. I tried to assure him that his fate would be a happier one than he had tried to imagine."

"But what was it, my child?" asked Sir William, drawing Ella upon his knee. His voice trembled, and upon his countenance were shades of fear.

"Can you not guess, father?"

"I would rather you should tell me."

"Then I will, for surely I could wish to keep nothing from my father. Alfred has confessed to me—no, no—I made him tell me—that he loved me, and he feared that you would reject him. But I knew that you —— What ails you, father?"

"Oh, my child, in my simple trust I did not think of this!" exclaimed the old man, trembling violently.

"Did not think of what, father?"

"Of this thing that has happened."

"But what is it? Surely you misunderstand me," returned Ella, drawing her arm about her parent's neck. "I told you that Alfred loved me—that he loved me with his whole noble, generous and pure soul; and God knows how fondly I love him in return. Oh, I knew I could assure him that you were too kind to refuse him my hand. I knew you would not refuse me the happiest boon I could ask on earth."

"And did you assure him all this?"

"Certainly. But what makes you look so strangely, father? What makes you tremble so? Oh, heaven forbid that I have done aught to pain you!"

"Alas! my child, you know not what you have done. I was a fool to leave you thus; but I thought you would look upon each other only as brother and sister. Ella, this can never be."

"Oh, you mean not that! You do not mean that I may not be the wife of Alfred?"

"It cannot be. I will do anything for your happiness, anything for your comfort; but I cannot do this!"

"Why, why, oh, why?"
"Do not ask me now!"
"Is not Alfred noble and good?"
"Yes."
"Is he not virtuous?"
"Yes."
"Is he not just and honorable?"
"Yes."
"Is he not well educated and gentlemanly?"
"Yes."
"And did he not snatch me from the hand of death, when no one else was by to give me succor?"
"Yes."
"And has he not a right to love me, in that he it was who planted in my mind seeds of pure and holy thought; who first led me to a knowledge of my God and my Saviour?"
"I cannot deny it."
"Then what shall now keep us asunder? Is it because he is poor? because"——

"Stop, stop, my child," cried the old man, in tones of agony. "You know not all you have to fear. I cannot tell you now, for I must see and converse with Alfred. O God, would that he had never come to my home! I did not think of this, I did not think of it!"

Ella was now moved more by the strange agony of her aged parent than she was by the thought of what he had said, and throwing her arms about his neck, she imparted a warm kiss upon his cheek.

"There, my sweet child, go to your room now. Oh, heaven grant that this blow fall not heavily upon you. Bear up, Ella, for your own sake, for my sake, try to forget what has passed."

The girl took a step towards the door, and then she stopped. She turned her tearful eyes upon her father, she tottered forward, and again sank upon his bosom.

"Oh, my father, I cannot bear this! Do not tear my heart thus from its early, only love!"

"Leave me now," the old man uttered. "I will see you again."

The stricken girl retired to her room, and the admiral fell almost senseless into a seat.

CHAPTER XXI.

THE NIGHT OF LIFE GROWS DARKER YET.

On the following morning Ella did not come down to breakfast as usual. Sir William looked sad and heavy-hearted, and Alfred was full of fear and trembling. He had vague forebodings of evil, and he thought that the sea of bitter trial was again in to open its tempestuous passage for him.

Early in the forenoon, while Sir William and our hero were in one of the lower drawing-rooms, where they had sat for half an hour in utter silence, one of the servants handed the baronet a card.

"Show him in," said the old man, as he read the name upon the missive.

It was an elderly gentleman who was introduced, and he wore the uniform of a surgeon in the royal navy. He was presented to our hero as Doctor Robert Holland.

"Harrold, did you say, Sir William?" asked the doctor, as he gazed into Alfred's face.

The doctor pulled the old admiral one side, and for some moments they conversed in a low whisper.

Holland started across the room as soon as he had done whispering, and a dozen times did he pace the length of the room with quick, nervous strides.

"Why, what has possessed you, doctor?" asked Sir William, in surprise.

"Oh, nothing," returned Holland; and as he answered he sank into a chair, took up a book, opened it bottom upwards, and then began to toss his foot in a strange manner.

The baronet regarded him for some moments in silence.

"Doctor," he said at length, "will you excuse me a few moments?"

"Medicine chest isn't here."

"I say, will you excuse me for a short time?"

"Excuse—eh? You haven't done anything wrong."

"You don't understand me," uttered Sir William, not a little puzzled by the doctor's actions. "I wish to leave you for a while."

"Ah—oh—yes, yes—now I see. Yes, yes," said the surgeon, arousing from his deep reverie. "You can go. Yes, yes, I'll stay until you come back."

The baronet beckoned for Alfred to follow him, and then turning from the room he led the way to the library. When once there he closed the door, and having bid the young man to be seated, he sank into his own great chair.

Several times Sir William seemed on the point of speaking, but his words did not come forth. Minutes passed away, and yet the two cast occasional glances at each other—nervous, uneasy glances—without saying a word. The silence was becoming oppressive, and at length the old man spoke.

"Alfred," he said, in a tone of deep feeling and anxiety, "the hour has come in which I must be plain with you. It would give me pain to be the instrument of unhappiness to you, but when you know all, you will not, cannot blame me. I conversed with Ella last evening, and she told me all that had transpired between you. That subject upon which you dwelt must go no farther. My child can never be more to you than she is now. Perhaps I was to blame for leaving you and Ella together, but I did not hold a suspicion that there would arise between you any other feelings than those which a brother and sister might feel."

"Pardon me, Sir William," returned the youth, with a look and tone in which were shadowed forth all the anguish of that aching heart. "I could not keep back the fond love that for so many years has been the sunlight of my dreary path. I could not hide from Ella the heart that must be ever hers. But I know I may never be in the happy possession of her hand. I am too poor, too humble for such aspirations."

"Ah, Alfred! you misunderstand me. Poverty and humble birth weigh not against you. Oh, it is something deeper than that."

The young man started, and again that deadly pallor overspread his features. His breath came heavy and quick, and his head was bowed. When he looked up, his features had grown calmer—the muscles had assumed a rigid expression—the thin lips were almost colorless, and the deep blue eyes were swimming in a sort of painful glare.

"Sir William," he said, in a tone of strange, unnatural calmness, "do you know the story of my family—of my earliest life?"

"Yes."

"Then I would bear it."

"I will tell you all, Alfred, all; and then you will know why I have done as I have. Your father was Sir John Lanford, and he was a rear admiral in our navy."

"Can it be so?" ejaculated the youth, closing his eyes and sinking back. "Now I know it all; but go on, sir."

"Your father and myself were brought up together from childhood. We were midshipmen together, and together we passed through the various grades till we were both admirals. Sir John had command of a fleet in the Mediterranean during the last French war, and he surrendered his own ship into the hands of the French at Toulon. He did it without striking hardly a blow in defence; and for doing it he received from the French government one hundred thousand pounds."

"Oh, mercy!" groaned Alfred.

"He received it in promissory notes and drafts signed and sealed by the French minister. This business was done very secretly, but such a remarkable piece of work could not remain a secret. The French minister told the story of his dealings with Sir John, and in a very short time our own government got hold of the matter. An exchange of prisoners was quickly made, and the admiral was brought home and tried. In a small department of one of his chests were found the notes of the French minister, and also all the letters he had received from the enemy. These letters were all of them genuine, bearing the unmistakable hand and seal of the Frenchman, and the guilt was too apparent to admit of even a doubt. Shortly before this trial Sir John received news of the death of his wife. All about him was dark and sunless, and he made but a feeble plea for innocence. Of course he was found guilty of the most dangerous species of high treason, and condemned to be hanged. After his condemnation, he barely answered when spoken to, offering no assertions of innocence. He asked to be hung on shipboard, and the request was granted. I had to attend the execution. I saw him hanged, and I saw his corpse consigned to the deep grave of the ocean. He had begged that he might be thus buried."

"Oh, terrible!" groaned Alfred.

"It was hard," resumed Sir William, while the big tears rolled down his furrowed cheeks; "it was hard; but it may have been just. Before your father died he made me promise that he would look after his child, then but a year old. I went to Gloucester, whither it had been carried, but I found that the little boy had gone. The people told me that two men had come and taken him, and that they came with a written order from Sir John himself. By the description I received, I knew they must have been Marrok Pettrell and Mark Bronkon, two petty officers who had belonged on board your father's ship, and who had been quite conspicuous at the trial.

"When I met you, four years ago in Cumberland, I knew you at once, and if I had a doubt, it was put at rest when you told me your story. Then I meant to have helped you, out of the love I bore your father; but now I owe the debt to you. I have obtained you a commission in the navy, but you must still bear the name of Harrold. The name of your father is sunk in"——

"Stop! stop!" cried Alfred, springing to his feet. "Heap not more infamy upon my father's name, for by the Judge of all things, I believe he was innocent."

"It was hard, Alfred, to believe him guilty; but so the world must ever hold him. Can you wonder now that I could not link my daughter's name with your own?"

"No, no, Sir William. I am used to misfortune, and I have schooled myself to bear it. This earth has no happiness for me. Since the first moment of my childho[od's] memory I have pursued the path of honor with unwavering footsteps. I have courted virtue with the whole ardor of my soul; and though sin has set against me in wild tempests of fearful power, yet never have I turned a single step with its flood. But misery is mine. I was born to it, and it must be my lot. I do not blame you, sir."

A moment the youth hesitated. Then his eye sparkled—his bosom heaved, and with strange vehemence he exclaimed:—

"But by heavens! sir, my father was an innocent man! Oh, why were those papers snatched from me!"

"Papers!" repeated the baronet.

"Yes, yes—papers which Mark Bronkon gave me." And Alfred related the circumstances as the reader already knows them.

When he had concluded, Sir William arose from his seat and began to pace the floor. When he stopped, it was directly in front of the youth, and there was an expression of more than common anxiety upon his features.

"Would to God I could have seen those papers," he uttered. "But I do not see how he could have been innocent. He must have had a hand in the affair, for on that night there was not a sentry on post. On board that ship, anchored within thirteen miles of an enemy's heavy battery, there were but one or two men on deck, and even they gave no alarm when the enemy's boats came alongside. Yet I would that I could have seen those papers."

"They are lost now! Lost forever!" murmured Alfred, burying his face in his hands.

A long silence ensued, which was at length broken by the baronet.

"Alfred," he said, "you must promise me that you will not think of Ella again in any other light than that of a friend."

"Anything; I can promise anything now," returned the youth, in a tone of utter dejection. "Anything of earth I can now give up without another pang. The death-angel alone can lift me to enjoyment again. Go, sir—go tell Ella all. Tell her to pray for me sometimes, and to think of me as one who loved her truly and well. You will not forget that I—I"——

The poor youth choked with emotion. He lifted his eyes towards the old man, and with a faint murmur upon his lips—a murmur that bore no palpable word upon its breath—he turned and left the room.

Sir William would have followed him, but he could not—he was too much overcome. When he did at length arise to go, he was met by his daughter.

"Where is Alfred?" she asked.

"He has just left me, my child."

"And what did you tell him? Oh, you did not refuse him as you did me. You told him that he might stay and make me happy; that I might be his own Ella forever. You did, did you not, my father?"

The old man sank back into his seat entirely overcome by this fresh attack upon his already weeping soul. It was a long time before he could answer; but at length he whispered into Ella's ear the whole tale of Alfred's misfortune, and of the ignominy that hung about his name.

"And must he suffer for this?" exclaimed the fair girl, with an earnestness her father had little expected. "Oh, my father, has not Alfred already suffered enough? Let me go to him. Let me go and pour the balm of peace over his tortured soul. He was ever noble—ever good to me. He loves me fondly, devotedly. Oh, let me go!"

"Hush, my child. You know not what you ask. Look forth upon the world, upon the future, and see my child linked for life with the child of one who was publicly hanged!"

"The world! The future!" repeated Ella, with a heaving bosom. "I carry my world and my future in my own soul. Oh, lay not the blame of a father's crime at the door of the suffering son. Let us rather bless him with the love-light of our kind smiles. Oh, we can make him happy! It lays in our power to make his life all bright and joyous. Shall we refuse?"

"O Ella, you know not what you ask. Say no more—say no more, or I shall suffer more than I can bear. If you would not see your poor father's head brought in sorrow to the grave, think of this thing no more."

Sir William was kind, but his family pride was strong. Ella knew it, and she felt that he would not bend.

"God have mercy on him!" the poor girl ejaculated. "He will have no home now."

"Yes, yes, my child. I have already provided a good place for him."

"Alas! I fear he will not accept it. But let us go and find him. Let me at least see him once more."

Sir William started up from his seat. A sudden thought flashed across his mind that Alfred might have left the house. He had not thought of such a thing before, but now the fear came upon him. He left the library and descended to the drawing-room, but Alfred was not there. He went to the hall, and the youth's hat was gone.

"Father, he has gone!" murmured the fair girl, as she leaned her head upon the bosom of her parent.

The old man had no word to say. His brain reeled and he tottered back, and with his child upon his bosom he sank down upon a fauteuil that stood against the wall. He felt that the youth to whom he owed the life of his daughter had fled from him, and that he had gone forth with new misery in his soul. He thought of his child, too; and he groaned in the heaviness of his grief.

CHAPTER XXII.

THE FIRST STREAK OF DAWN.

WITH a dizzy, aching head, Alfred hastened away from the dwelling of Sir William Brent. He could not stay there and feel the degradation which had fallen upon him. With hurried steps he moved on, and at length he turned towards the churchyard in Westminster, where Bronkon had told him his mother was buried. He reached the place, and easily gained access to the yard. He found a white marble block—a simple, plain memento—and on it read:—

"CAROLINE, wife of Sir John Landford, Bart."

Alfred leaned against the cold stone, and the warm tears flowed freely forth. He sank down upon his knees, and his heart felt lighter when he had prayed. Once more he had resolved to walk straight on in the path of duty, though that path might seem dark as utter night.

Over an hour did the youth remain in that home of the mouldering dead; and when he at length turned his steps away, the tears had been dried from his face, but his heart was sad. He knew not which way to turn, for he had no home, no destination on earth. He turned to take one more look upon the churchyard, and then he moved away.

He took his course towards the river, but ere he had gained the piers he was startled by hearing his own name pronounced. He looked around, and near him saw an oldish-looking man with a gray beard and slouched hat, who was closely regarding him. Our hero again started to pass on, when the stranger called to him a second time.

"Alfred," said the man.

"That's my name," returned the youth, utterly unable to recognize the man who had called him.

"Just come with me," said the stranger.

"For what?"

"I will tell you something you would like to know."

"But first I should like to know you."

"That wouldn't do you any good. Come with me, and you shall have reason to thank me."

Alfred still hesitated. He had never seen the man before, that he could remember, and, besides, he looked rough and uninviting.

"Tell me who you are, and then I may go with you."

"I cannot tell you here; but just follow me a short distance, and you shall know what you ask, and more, too. Come."

"Tell me your business first. I know you not."

"Don't fool away your time too long, or you may lose what you might wish much to gain," said the stranger, with a show of impatience. "I will not reveal myself here in the street, but come to that old tavern there, where you see the sign of the pipe and tankard, and you shall know me. Come, if you choose."

As the man spoke he started towards the place pointed out. Alfred hesitated but a moment longer, and then he followed. He knew of no danger to apprehend. The stranger and our hero entered the tavern together. It was a dirty place, and in the taproom were some dozen villanous-looking fellows engaged in smoking and drinking. Alfred's companion beckoned to the greasy publican and asked for a private room. The fellow moved his corpulent body with wonderful alacrity, seeming to look upon the stranger with a deferential air, and soon the room was provided.

The man turned the key in the lock of the door, and then turned towards our hero.

"Alfred, don't you know me?"

"I do not remember you," returned the youth, vainly endeavoring to call to mind some scene in which a man with such looks had borne a part.

"Ha, ha, ha! I shall feel safe now," uttered the fellow; and he pulled the gray beard from his face.

"Callum!" uttered our hero, in blank astonishment.

"Paul Callum, at your service," returned the escaped pirate. "You don't wonder that I keep close, do you? Poor fellows are we who dare not look honest men in the face. But that don't matter now. I've been dodging about Lunnun these three weeks, trying to get a sight of you, and now you've hove in sight. Tell me, Alfred, didn't ye lose something when you were cast away on the Cornwall coast?"

"Lose?—yes, yes!" cried the youth.

"What was it?"

"A package."

"Done up in oiled silk?"

"Yes, yes."

"Well, don't look so frightened, for I happened to find it."

"And have you got it with you?"

"Of course I have."

"Safe?—safe? Let me see it, Paul; let me see it!"

"That's it," returned Callum, drawing the package from his bosom. "It hasn't been opened. There it is, just as I found it, and you shall have it once more. I have took some trouble, and run some dangers, to get this back to you, but you were always good and kind to me; you taught me to read and write, and perhaps I've now done you a service in return. When we were cast away, the captain and Bill Grinnell and me, all three of us, come ashore in the bunt of the mainsail. You know, of course, that the mainmast was over the stern all the while. We wasn't hurt hardly any. In the morning I heard the captain tell Bill that he wanted to find your body, for he believed Bronkon had given you something that you hadn't ought to have had. I found you first clean up to the head of the beach, and the package was half way out of your bosom. Grabbing it, I slipped it into my bosom, just as Pettrell came up. I believed you would come to life, so I determined to hang on to the package till I could get it into your hands. I had to run, then; but I've found you now, and I hope I've done you some service."

"Service!" repeated Alfred, as he grasped the package, which he saw had not been opened; "you've done me more of good than even the saving of my life. How can I repay you?"

"You have more than repaid me now. All I ask is that you won't betray me. Pettrell will swing, and I know he deserves it. Bill Grinnell has gone to the States and I shall follow him."

"You have nothing to fear from me, Paul; and if I can assist you in any way I will do it. Have you got money enough?"

"Yes, plenty."

"Then I can only thank you for your favor, and pray that God will henceforth help you to lead an honest life."

"Ah, Alfred, that I am determined to do. I have tried the path of evil just long enough to find that there is no peace for the mind, nor real good for the body, in it. A poor fellow may make a little money now and then; but what good can it do him when he can't bless himself with it? No, no; there is no more of this dark life for me. I'll go where I'm not known, and there I'll commence anew. I'm not too old to reform, and I have not been so wicked but that I may find some real happiness in it yet."

As Callum spoke, he replaced the gray beard upon his face, and then arose from his seat."

"Give me your hand, Alfred. There, God bless you for all the kindness you have done for me; and if ever I learn to pray with an honest heart, you shall be the first man I pray for."

"God bless you, too, Paul," exclaimed our hero, as he returned the fellow's warm grasp. "You shall find often a place in my prayers."

"Thank you, thank you, Alfred. And now let's be off. I'm bound now for Gravesend. I may never see you again; so good-by."

Alfred shook Callum's hand again, and having once more gained the street, they separated, the latter hastening off towards the river, while the former stood and watched him until he was out of sight.

"Oh, mysterious package!" murmured the youth, as he pressed the same to his bosom; "God grant that you contain the wand that shall remove the stain from my father's name! I'll to Sir William's once more, and he shall see whether my house is foul or fair. Ella, I may never reach thee, but I shall be nearer to thee, at least."

With these words trembling upon his lips, the youth quickened his pace. The sun was just sinking from sight when he entered Hanover Square, and with a strangely beating heart he ascended the steps that led to the baronet's door and rang the bell.

CHAPTER XXIII.
THE SEAL BROKEN—THE LIFE BOOK OPENED.

As Alfred entered the drawing-room and sank into a seat, "Thank heaven that you have come back to me," Sir William fervently ejaculated; "I feared that you had left this place never to return." -

"I intended, Sir William, never to have crossed your threshold again, for I could not dwell beneath the same roof with one I so wildly loved, and who was yet shut out from me forever. But an unexpected event has for the present changed my plans. I have recovered those papers, sir, of which I spoke to you."

"Papers?" repeated Sir William.

"Those, sir, which Mark Bronkon gave me, and which may yet prove that my father was innocent."

Doctor Holland who sat in the same room, started from his chair in astonishment.

"Papers that Bronkon gave you?" he uttered. "Innocent, did you say? Sir John Landford innocent?"

"Let the papers speak for themselves," said Sir William.

"Here they are. You shall open them," said Alfred, as with a trembling hand he drew the package from his bosom and passed it to the baronet.

Sir William took the package and then having summoned one of his servants, he called for lamps. When they were brought, the curtains were drawn over the windows, and the parties drew their chairs up to the table. Alfred trembled like an aspen, for a single stroke of the knife was to tell his doom. The baronet cut the string, and revealed quite a bundle of neatly folded papers.

The first was directed to Alfred, and Sir William read aloud, as follows:--

"ALFRED:—Accompanying this you will find a full statement of all the circumstances connected with that fatal affair which ended in your father's ignominious death. God knows that he was innocent, yet he suffered. The confession I wrote shortly after you saved my life off the coast of Lancashire, not then having fully made up my mind to give it to you. But now I have resolved to make all the reparation that lies in my power. Some things that concern myself I cannot write;

but I shall tell them to you if ever I give you the papers. I refer to the relations existing between myself and the fair being who gave you birth. When you open this package, you had better seek out Sir William Brent, in Hanover Square, London. He was your father's best friend, and he may help you. Forgive me the part I took against you, for God knows I have long since repented of it. BRONKON."

"Let's see! let's see!" quickly and nervously uttered Sir William. "Oh, if they but prove that Sir John was innocent, then his son shall at least receive the blessing!"

The next paper was opened, and it was addressed to Alfred, but also bore a recommendation to "All friends of Sir John Landford." The baronet opened it and read:—

"ALFRED:—Of course you must know that you are no son of Marrok Pettrell; but you are, in fact, the child of Sir John Landford, Rear Admiral, who was hanged on board the 'Sussex,' for high treason. But of that crime your father was wholly innocent, Pettrell and myself being the prime movers in the affair. Four years before that event Sir John tried a man for mutiny on board his own ship, and had him hanged. That man was Marrok Pettrell's brother, and from that moment Marrok swore to be revenged. He found me a ready tool to work with him, for I was just smarting under the wound I had received in the loss of one whom I loved as my own life, and who married the admiral. I may sometime explain this more fully."

Here Alfred had to relate to Sir William and the doctor what Bronkon had told him when he gave him the package. Then the baronet resumed his reading.

"Marrok and myself both shipped on Sir John's vessel, and it was not long before a most extraordinary opportunity was offered for carrying our plan into execution. We were anchored off the harbor of Toulon, whither we had gone to regain two of our Indiamen that had been captured by the French. Pettrell had been appointed boatswain's mate, and one day while off in one of the boats after a spare spar that had got afloat, he was hailed by a French officer who had come out in a sail-boat. The officer came alongside and gave Pettrell a letter, which he requested might be given to the admiral, at the same time stating that he should be there on the next day, at the same hour, for an answer. The very nature of the circumstances opened Pettrell's mind to a strange suspicion. As soon as he returned to the ship he drew me one side and showed me the letter. We broke the seal and found it to be a proposition from the French commander, offering to Sir John the sum of one hundred thousand pounds if he would quietly surrender the ship into their hands.

"The letter was again folded up, and the seal melted together, and Pettrell went to the cabin and delivered it to the admiral. In the meantime I obtained some of Sir John's chirography, and then sat down and wrote an answer to the Frenchman's letter, partially accepting his proposition, but requiring more definite terms. To this I affixed the admiral's signature, and then sealed and directed it. As we had hoped, on the next day, Sir John handed to Pettrell a letter in answer to the one he had received the previous day, and directed him to deliver it to the officer of whom he had received the note. The letter I had written was delivered, and the admiral's own letter was retained by us! You will find it in the package. It is numbered 'two!'"

"Let's see it," faintly uttered Doctor Holland.

It was taken from the package, and read as follows:—

"H. B. M. Ship "Medusa."

"Monsieur ——:—I received from you a proposition offering me a bribe for the safe and quiet delivery into your hands of my ship. I am an Englishman! That should be answer enough; but if you will come forth on your errand, I will give you a more substantial answer in the shape of powder and cold iron.

"With the utmost contempt, I am your enemy, JOHN LANDFORD, BART."

"The old admiral himself!" cried Sir William, as his eyes filled with tears.

"O God!" murmured Alfred, "and that letter was kept back, and another, a base forgery, sent in its place!"

"Yes," said Holland, "but read on."

Sir William wiped his eyes, and then he read again:—

"After this we managed to get six more letters from the Frenchman, all of them directed to the admiral, but not one of which he ever saw until they were produced against him as evidence of his guilt. Pettrell framed rough drafts for the answers, which you will find in the package, in his own uncouth hand. These I copied, addressed to the French commander, always signing Sir John's name. The Frenchman secured his letters in a small black box, not larger than a pipe-bowl, which he fastened to one corner of the buoy, where Pettrell took it when he rowed around in the morning to square the yards, and where he also left the answer we had prepared — the Frenchman, you understand, always coming at night.

"At length matters were all arranged, and the night was set on which the ship was to be surrendered, and yet we were not suspected, nor did the Frenchman suspect that Marrok Pettrell was not a bona-fide agent of the admiral. We had received notes of hand, or rather drafts on a heavy bank in Toulon, for the hundred thousand pounds, which were to be cashed as soon as presented, all payable to Sir John Landford. By means of our French agent we obtained a large quantity of a very powerful sedative —a sort of quintessent extract of henbane and opium—which we mixed with the tea of the ship's company, and which we also contrived to get into the drink of the officers. Thus were all hands under control.

"At midnight the enemy came off in boats. Pettrell and myself were on deck; but all the rest of the watch were sound asleep. Of course the ship was taken almost without a blow. Our men were nearly all too stupid to make any resistance. As soon as Sir John came out from his cabin, I rushed in and placed all the letters we had received from the French, together with the drafts, in a small till in one of his chests. As they were all addressed to the admiral, of course they had an overwhelming weight in evidence, as the contents of our own forgeries were all alluded to in them. This consummated our plan. We were all taken prisoners; but the Frenchmen must have been surprised when Sir John indignantly refused their money, and at the same time disclaimed all knowledge of the affair. However, they attributed it to his fear of detection.

"At length the affair leaked out, and our whole crew were exchanged and carried home to England, where Sir John was tried. The letters were found in his chest, and Pettrell and myself swore to having carried them to him from the French. I could at that time see what no one else seemed to notice—and that was, that the terrible blow had turned the ill-fated admiral's brain; and beneath the effects of that mental derangement he suffered all without much attempt at defence.

"As soon as Sir John was hanged, Pettrell and myself hastened off to Gloucester, and by means of a forged order from your father, we obtained possession of you—Pettrell having sworn that you, too, should be brought to the gallows, to make up the sum of his revenge.

"What more can I tell you that you do not already know? You were then one year old, and your mother had already been laid in her grave. Three years after that, while we were engaged in smuggling, our vessel was cast away on Little Devon Head, and you were lost to us for several years. How you were at length found you know.

"And now, God forgive me for the deed I hoped to consummate. I hope this will serve you. You need no advice from me, and I will give none. I can only swear most solemnly, before that God whose laws

I have so often outraged, that every word I have here written is true!

"MARK BRONKON."

As Sir William ceased reading, the paper dropped from his hand, and he sank back in his great chair. The surgeon started up and flew to and fro across the room like a crazy man. Alfred put forth his hand and laid it upon the baronet's arm, and in a low whisper he uttered:—

"Was not my father innocent?"

"Innocent!" repeated the baronet, starting up from his seat, and then sinking back again. "Oh, that fearful thought has never ceased to haunt me. A dark mystery always hung over that fatal scene in the closing life of my best friend. Everything seemed against him, and I was forced to believe him guilty; yet my soul, my heart, was never reconciled to the judgment. Innocent! Oh, poor Sir John!"

Holland stopped suddenly in his walk and seized the letter which Sir John had written to the Frenchman, and which the conspirators had kept back.

"'I am an Englishman!'" he read. "Oh, how like the old admiral. 'That should be answer enough!' O Sir John! 'If you will come forth on your errand, I will give you a more substantial answer in the shape of powder and cold iron!' What a precious document is this! 'With the utmost contempt, I am your enemy—JOHN LANDFORD.' O Sir William, he was innocent!"

The old baronet could only groan, and clasp his hands in agony. The other papers in the package were looked over, and they were found to be, as Bronkon had said, the rough drafts of the letters which had been written to the Frenchman over the forged signature of the admiral.

"Was not that a base conspiracy?" uttered Sir William, as he held the papers in his hand. "What a noble soul did England cast away when that man was so wrongfully put to death."

At that moment a servant opened the door and announced that there was a man at the door who wished to see Alfred.

"Then let him come in here," said the baronet. "Whatever interests Alfred now must also interest me."

The old man looked upon the youth as he spoke, and the latter returned a silent motion of consent.

CHAPTER XXIV.

CONCLUSION.

IT was an old man who entered the room—a man bent down beneath heavy burdens—"a man of sorrow and a man of grief." He stopped as he stood in the presence of those who were there assembled, and for a moment his frame shook like a frightened child.

"Alfred!" he at length murmured, "Alfred, my boy, I have come to see you once more."

The head of that old man was on the next instant pillowed upon the youth's bosom, and Alfred gently murmured the name of "Luke Garron!"

"Oh, my more than father!" cried our hero, as he clasped the old light-keeper more fondly within his arms, "God has sent you back to me. Sir William, this is now my father."

The baronet had sprung to his feet, for he recognized the man from whose hands he had received his daughter.

But oh, how was Luke Garron changed! That stout, noble form was bent; that glossy raven hair was all frosted like the driven snow; those features, once so full of the soul's life, were now in weeping for the soul's decay; those darkly flashing eyes were sunken, and their light was dimmed; those hands, once so strong, now trembled like stricken reeds, and he was all bowed and heart-broken.

"You shall never leave me more," uttered Alfred. "Henceforth our home shall be together. You protected me in childhood, and I will now watch over you in your old age."

"Bless you, bless you, my boy; but that may not be. My stop here cannot be long.

But where is Ella? Oh, I must see her sweet face once more."

Ella was sent for, and as she entered the room the first object that met her gaze was Alfred, and towards him she moved.

"No, no, Ella," said the youth, "not to me—not to me. Here."

He laid his hand upon Luke's arm as he spoke.

"Ella," uttered the old man, "do you not know me?"

The fair girl gazed up into his face, and on the next instant she was upon his bosom. She murmured his name—she blessed him—and she pressed her lips upon his deeply furrowed brow.

When Luke Garron sank back upon the large sofa that stood near him, his storm children were by his side.

"Doctor Holland," said Sir William, "this is the old light-keeper of whom you have heard me speak. An old friend of mine, Mr. Garron," added the baronet, turning towards Luke.

The old man turned his eyes upon the surgeon, and a deadly pallor overspread his features. He attempted to rise, but his limbs failed him, and he sank back upon his seat.

"Are you ill?" anxiously asked Ella, putting her arm around Luke's neck.

"No, my child, it was only a sudden weakness. Ah, I have such attacks often."

A short silence ensued, during which the doctor moved his chair nearer to where Luke sat. At length Sir William asked the old light-keeper where he had been since he had left the Devon beacon.

"I have sought you often," he said, "but could never gain any tidings of you."

"Alas!" murmured Luke, "I have had no home since that time. I have been a wanderer without destination."

"But you should have come and seen me," said the affectionate Ella.

"So I have seen you, sweet child. When you knew it not, I have stood and watched you."

"Ah, I saw you once on the opposite side of the square."

"Yes; I remember. I thought you detected me then, and I left my post."

"But you will stay with us now. Oh, my good father will give you a home."

"Yes," said Sir William; "your wanderings shall now have an end. Beneath my roof you shall find a home."

"No, no," groaned Luke; "it cannot be. I wished to see these children once again before I died; and now I have seen them. I must go now."

He caught the burning glance of Robert Holland, and tremblingly arose to his feet.

"O God!" he murmured, as he clasped his hands towards heaven, help me through this trial. Sir William, you will not turn poor Alfred from your doors. Be a father to him. Bless him with your love. Ella—Alfred—one more kiss. There, I must go! O God! I cannot bear this! My poor heart is weaker than I thought. Alfred! Alfred! God bless you! Sir William"—

"Stop, stop!" cried the old surgeon, springing from his chair, and grasping the light-keeper by the arm. "By my soul's salvation, I know you now!"

"Know me!" gasped the weak old man, shrinking with terror.

"Yes, yes. Sir John Landford, I know you well!"

"O God! Betrayed!—discovered!—ruined!" fell from the old man's lips, as he sank back upon the sofa.

"No, no, Sir John; none here shall betray you," exclaimed Holland.

Alfred heard these words—he heard the name of his father—his brain reeled, and with a dizzy sensation, he fell across the old man's knees. When he came to himself his father had lifted him up, and with a bursting heart he found utterance for his soul's thanksgiving.

It was some time ere Sir William recovered from the utter astonishment into which this wonderful revelation had thrown him.

"You wonder at this, Sir William," said the old surgeon, as he settled into his seat.

"Wonder?" repeated the baronet, gazing first upon Sir John, and then upon the doctor. "It is a miracle!"

"Upon my soul!" replied Holland, "I do believe the hand of God is in the work; but I can explain it all. If you remember, you grew sick at the sight of Sir John hanging at the yard-arm, and ordered him cut down sooner than might otherwise have been done. When he was taken below I saw a twitching of one of the muscles at the corner of the mouth. In an instant the thought struck me that life was not extinct. I had him carried to my room, and, having ordered all the attendants out, I locked the door, and then commenced operations upon the body. Life was there, and in half an hour Sir John sat up and spoke. He prayed for me to save him, and I resolved to do it; but I first made him promise that he would never reveal himself, even to his own child. His own safety as well as mine, required that; for were he to be found, he would again be hanged. I hastened on shore and bought a waxen figure of old Dame Rollins. This I carried off in a large chest. I was forced to let my steward into the secret; but I was not afraid to trust him. We sewed the waxen figure closely up in a hammock, putting in lead enough to make it as heavy as a dead body would be, and Sir John was carried on shore in the chest. No one thought of questioning the contents of the hammock, for it bore the stamp of the human form; and when it sank beneath the bosom of the closing waters, all, save myself and steward, thought that the cold corpse of Sir John was there. O Sir William, when I saw you weeping there, I wished that you could have known as much as I did; but I dared not reveal to you the secret. From that time till this evening I

A STARTLING DENOUEMENT.

have seen nothing of the man I saved, though when you first told me of Luke Garron, I suspected the truth."

"You will not betray me?" cried Sir John, as Doctor Holland concluded. "Let me go. I will now seek some"——

"Stop, my old friend," said Sir William, starting forward to the table. "O God is surely here. His finger marks every page of life! Sir John, you are innocent."

"God knows I am!"

"Yes, yes, and we know it. The world shall know it. Here—here, in three papers, have we your full acquittal. Sit down, sit down, Sir John."

The old man sank back to his seat, and then Sir William commenced to read the confession of Mark Bronkon, and while he read, Sir John Landford started back to life. His bosom heaved, his dark eyes sparkled with a glowing fire, his muscles worked with increasing power; and when the story was told, he sprang to his feet and lifted his hands high above his head. His form was straight, and his head once more erect. A full minute he stood thus, and then, as the tears rolled in torrents down his cheeks, he sank upon his knees, and the long pent-up prayer of his soul burst forth in glowing, burning words.

When he once more drew Alfred to his bosom, he told of the trials he had undergone since he fled from Portsmouth, where the doctor had set him free. He had found the light-house without a keeper, and he obtained the situation. He had learned that Pettrell had got possession of his child, but he dared not seek for it. When, three years afterwards, Alfred was washed on shore, the light-keeper knew him; and when the little fellow prattled of Marrok Pettrell, the fact was beyond a doubt.

The old man told him how life opened its joys to him again as he reared his fond child, and as that child learned to love him. He told of the coming of Pettrell, and his frame shook with a fearful tremor as he reverted to that scene. He dared not claim his own child as flesh of his flesh, for that would have doomed him to the fearful, terrible death he had once escaped, and he was forced to see the object of his heart's devotion torn from him.

The old man's heart bled afresh as he told of that parting, and his friends gathered about him to soothe and comfort him. Soon the cloud passed away, and Sir John opened his eyes upon the bliss of the present hour. Brent and Holland were bending fondly over him, while Alfred and Ella were clinging to his knees. The story of his grief had been told, and now his words were only thanks and blessings.

It was evening again, and the scene is again in the large drawing-room of Sir William Brent. But what a brilliant assemblage is there. The lords of the admiralty are there, and some of old England's bravest, battle-scarred heroes are there, too. The package which Bronkon had given Alfred had been read by the king, and Marrok Pettrell had confessed it all true, though at the time he dreamed not that his victim lived. Yet the pirate captain had made the confession, and he had since paid the penalty of his crimes with his life.

Sir John Landford was again a man among men. Upon his shoulders he bore the broad epaulets of a full admiral, and upon his bosom sparkled the insignia of the baronet.

There had just been feasting and joy upon the happy reunion of a noble Briton with his noble country; but now the voice of revelry is hushed. Sir John arose and stepped forth to where sat his son by the side of Sir William's daughter.

"Alfred—Ella," he said, as he took them both by the hand, "Sir William has granted me this happy privilege. I took you both to my bosom when you were helpless children, and I saw the vines of your young heart's affection twine softly, tenderly about each other. You were once given to me in the midst of storm and tempest, and then you were lost to me when the heaven was black in night. But now—now heaven has opened the light of full day upon us—and my STORM CHILDREN are mine once more. Alfred, you remember that dark night when we sat together in the old beacon? Then I told you never to turn aside from the true path of life. Nobly have you met the storms that have beset your way, and now you see how signally your faithful virtue has been blessed. Ella, you have found another father, but our laws provide that you may yet have two fathers. This act makes you my daughter still. There, she is yours, Alfred; and, Ella, I know you will take my son for your own with your whole soul."

As Sir John spoke, he laid Ella's hand

within that of Alfred, and then he turned away to wipe the happy tears from his face.

Sir William stepped forward and laid his hands upon the heads of Alfred and Ella.

"Oh," he murmured, as he met the joyful looks of those two re-united beings, "how little can they know of true joy who have no blessing to impart to those about them. Surely there is more real pleasure in making some fellow creature happy, than mere self can ever find in the sensual wealth of earth. Oh, give me ever the smiles of happy friends about me, and I can ask no more."

WILLIAM H. THOMES,

THE CELEBRATED

Australian and Californian Adventurer.

LATEST AND BEST WORKS.

THE BELLE OF AUSTRALIA;
     Or, Who Am I?
ON LAND AND SEA;
    Or, California in 1843. '44, '45.
LEWEY AND I;
    Or, Sailor Boys' Wanderings.

ALL HANDSOMELY BOUND IN CLOTH & GILT.

$1.50 PER VOLUME, POST-PAID.

DEWOLFE, FISKE & CO., Publishers,

365 WASHINGTON ST., BOSTON, MASS.

BALLOU'S MONTHLY MAGAZINE.

AN ILLUSTRATED LITERARY MAGAZINE FOR THE FAMILY.

ENTERTAINING, INSTRUCTIVE, AND AMUSING READING.

A FIRST CLASS PUBLICATION.

PRICE, $1.50 PER YEAR, POST-PAID.

CLUB TERMS.— Four copies, $5.00. Additions to club pro rata, price, $1.25 each post-paid. For sale by all Newsdealers. Price, 15 cents. Specimen copies sent to any address on receipt of ten cents. No notice taken of postal cards calling for sample copies.

THE NOVELETTES.

For $2 we will send BALLOU'S MAGAZINE for 1886, and either five of our BRILLIANT NOVELETTES, all post-paid; and for $2.50 we will send BALLOU'S MAGAZINE and ten of our BRILLIANT NOVELETTES, all post-paid.

☞ For $2.50 we will send a copy of either "THE BELLE OF AUSTRALIA," "ON LAND AND SEA," or "LEWEY AND I," elegantly bound in cloth and gold, and BALLOU'S MONTHLY MAGAZINE for one year; two books and Magazine, $3.75; or all three books and Magazine for $5.00.

GEORGE W. STUDLEY, Publisher.

23 HAWLEY ST., BOSTON, MASS.

THE NOVELETTE.

No. 1. The Arkansas Ranger, or Dingle the Backwoodsman.
A STORY OF EAST AND WEST. BY LIEUTENANT MURRAY.
A vivid story, unrivaled in plot and character; thrilling in marvelous adventures.

No. 2. The Sea Lion, or The Privateer of the Penobscot.
A STORY OF OCEAN LIFE. BY SYLVANUS COBB, JR.
One of Cobb's best; occurring during that fertile period of adventure, our second war with England.

No. 3. Marion's Brigade, or The Light Dragoons.
A TALE OF THE REVOLUTION. BY DR. J. H. ROBINSON.
Among the many tales which our Revolutionary struggles have drawn from the pens of noted historians and story-tellers, perhaps none excel this one from the pen of Dr. Robinson.

No. 4. Bessie Baine, or The Mormon's Victim.
A TALE OF UTAH. BY M. QUAD, OF THE *DETROIT FREE PRESS.*
In this great original story, written expressly for our establishment, Mr. Lewis has shown up the whole system of Mormonism, and all its terrible aims and results.

No. 5. The Red Revenger, or The Pirate King of the Floridas.
A TALE OF THE GULF AND ITS ISLANDS. BY NED BUNTLINE.
This thrilling tale is one that portrays many tragic and romantic phases of life at a period when deadly conflict was maintained between the Spaniards of Cuba and the desperate pirates who infested the seas in its vicinity some three centuries ago.

No. 6. Orlando Chester, or The Young Hunter of Virginia.
A STORY OF COLONIAL TIMES. BY SYLVANUS COBB, JR.
This story is one of the happiest efforts of the author, who has wrought out a series of domestic scenes in private life of much interest.

No. 7. The Secret-Service Ship, or The Fall of San Juan d'Ulloa.
A ROMANCE OF THE MEXICAN WAR. BY CAPT. CHARLES E. AVERILL.
The author enjoyed extraordinary facilities for gaining the actual knowledge necessary to the production of his captivating story; and hence its truthfulness and excellence.

No. 8. Adventures in the Pacific, or In Chase of a Wife.
BY COL. ISAAC H. FOLGER.
This sea story will attract much attention from residents of the Cape, and many old whaling captains and crews will recall its characters and incidents with lively interest, and all fond of adventure will read it with relish.

No. 9. Ivan the Serf, or The Russian and Circassian.
A TALE OF RUSSIA, TURKEY, AND CIRCASSIA. BY AUSTIN C. BURDICK.
This is a well-told and highly graphic story of life, domestic and military, in Russia, Turkey, and Circassia.

No. 10. The Scout, or The Sharpshooters of the Revolution.
A STORY OF OUR REVOLUTIONARY STRUGGLE. BY MAJOR BEN. PERLEY POORE.
This story of our Revolutionary struggle is one of much interest, and narrates, with vivid, lifelike effect, some of the scenes of that eventful period.

No. 11. Daniel Boone, or The Pioneers of Kentucky.
AN HISTORICAL ROMANCE OF EARLY WESTERN LIFE. BY DR. J. H. ROBINSON.
The terrible experiences of the early Western settlers, with their perils and privations, their struggles and their triumphs, afford a vivid field for the writer, who has lent himself to the task with a rich result.

No. 12. The King of the Sea.
A TALE OF THE FEARLESS AND FREE. BY NED BUNTLINE.
This is one of the most popular romances of the sea written by this well-known author, and the characters which appear are replete with interest and individuality.

No. 13. The Queen of the Sea, or Our Lady of the Ocean.
A TALE OF LOVE AND CHIVALRY. BY NED BUNTLINE.
This is a story of the buccaneers or the seventeenth century, and is fraught with the sanguinary incidents of those times.

No. 14. The Heart's Secret, or The Fortunes of a Soldier.
A TALE OF LOVE AND THE LOW LATITUDES. BY LIEUTENANT MURRAY.
This is a very interesting story of life among the noble in the island of Cuba. Its plot is well conceived and happily carried out, and furnishes a skilful series of events of intense interest.

No. 15. The Storm Children, or The Light-Keeper of the Channel.
A STORY OF LAND AND SEA ADVENTURE. BY SYLVANUS COBB, JR.
This story is one of great interest. The principal incidents are located on the coast of England, although the developments carry the reader into the Eastern world. It is a fine portraiture of human character.

FOR SALE BY ALL NEWSDEALERS, Price Fifteen Cents, or sent post-paid on receipt of price.

GEORGE W. STUDLEY, PUBLISHER, 23 HAWLEY STREET, BOSTON, MASS.

www.ingramcontent.com/pod-product-compliance
Lightning Source LLC
Chambersburg PA
CBHW020332090426
42735CB00009B/1507